Following the Lamb

Christina Le Moignan

Following the Lamb

*A Reading of Revelation
for the New Millennium*

EPWORTH PRESS

0 7162 0537 8

First published 2000
by Epworth Press
20 Ivatt Way
Peterborough, PE3 7PG

Typeset by Regent Typesetting, London
Printed and bound in Great Britain by Biddles Ltd,
Guildford and King's Lynn

Contents

Acknowledgments

The work for this book began during sabbatical leave from my post as Tutor at the Queen's College, Birmingham, and much of the writing was completed during a sabbatical offered to me as a Methodist minister by the Methodist Church. I am grateful both to the College and the Church for making this time available, as I am to the trustees of the Fernley Hartley Trust for their invitation to give the Fernley Hartley Lecture of 1996 on the subject of this book. The material in the lecture has been considerably expanded here, particularly in Part Two of the book. I owe much also to the encouragement of friends and colleagues, and especially to those who have read the book in draft form and made helpful suggestions, as well as to those who have advised about the production of the script.

My concern that Christian faith should be more than private was largely formed during my time as a tutor at Queen's, and I acknowledge gladly my debt to the Queen's community in this respect. Many teachers have inspired and enabled me in my study of the New Testament, and I thank them all. Most fundamentally I am in debt to the Christian family, largely but by no means exclusively Methodist, among whom I have learned that following the Lamb is what life is about. I owe most here to my mother and father, to whose memory this book is dedicated in love and gratitude.

Preface

This book is an invitation. First, it is an invitation to open a part of the Bible which many people think of as difficult and dangerous, and so prefer to keep closed. Revelation is neither simple nor risk-free, but it is eminently worth reading. For, more than any other New Testament book, it is concerned with the world, and what the world is coming to. Many Christians today share that concern, but are not sure what to do with it. The problems seem too big. So people retreat, though with a sense of unease, into the certainties of God's love for themselves and others as individuals. But what if this little-read book has a way out of 'privatized religion' into Christian faith lived for the world? *Following the Lamb* is an invitation to consider that possibility, and to allow our tentative questioning to be confronted by Revelation's urgent call to faithfulness.

The book begins with a sketch of some of the challenges that the world presents as we enter the third millennium. Part One introduces Revelation, giving an outline of its contents, suggesting a way of reading it, and arguing for its validity as a vision for Christians today. Part Two then explores how Revelation may help us see today's world, discusses what acting on its vision might mean, and presents Revelation's call to 'follow the Lamb'.

Following the Lamb has been written primarily for what John and Charles Wesley would have called 'practical believers'. Some readers may find it easiest to move from the introductory chapter straight to Part Two, since that is where the issues of daily life in today's world and church are raised. But of course the book will have failed in its intention if Revelation itself is not read, and it is at that point that Part One is offered, not as a commentary (which is far beyond the scope of this book), but as a travel guide to the practical believer in unfamiliar and even alien territory.

This book is avowedly incomplete, even for practical believers, let alone for those who would like to explore Revelation from other points of view. The book raises as sharply as it can some major issues for today's Western Christians, but there is no complete list here of all the issues, far less are there answers to all the questions that they raise. What is offered, rather, is an invitation to the reader to share a vision. And an invitation to see where that vision leads.

INTRODUCTION

I

The Challenge of the New Millennium

'What *is* the world coming to?' That question could be merely the picturesque expression of a mild disquiet, but, at the time of the millennium, it could be a much more serious enquiry. We are creatures of time, and we number our days. Birthdays for individuals, anniversaries for couples, or for churches or nations, are invitations to take stock of the past and to look forward to the future. How much more is the millennium – two thousand years for the whole world since the birth of Christ – an irresistible invitation to ask the question: where are we, and where are we going? More than that, so signifi-cant a date raises questions about time itself. Is time going anywhere? What will happen to the universe at the end of time, if there is such a thing? And, is there any telling when the end might come? We may have been brought up to regard end-of-the-world prophecies with suspicion – but nonetheless we may find ourselves sneaking a look at some of the more lurid offerings in the bookshops 'just for interest'. For who cannot, at some deep level, be interested in what will happen to the world?

To ask any questions about the future is to confront our-selves with uncertainty, and human beings find uncertainty hard to bear. Of course the future may hold much promise. Who knows what secrets of the universe we may unlock in the twenty-first century, when even quite ordinary people may take their holidays in space? Who knows what new and

exciting knowledge or experience we might access on the
Internet? What might life be like free of the scourge of cancer,
or Alzheimer's Disease – or of hunger, when genetically modified crops have made crop failures a thing of the past? Yet, as
the mention of GM crops immediately signals, we are not
always sure whether we are dealing with promise or threat.
Perhaps GM crops will mean not an end to food shortages but
instead frightening environmental damage and the ruination
of farmers in poor countries in hock to agribusiness. For we
have our doubts about 'progress'. Antibiotics, we are now
learning, have costs and not just benefits. Nuclear power we
have seen used for peaceful purposes, but also for a destruction that we cannot bear to think about. Of the hundreds of
different television channels that will be on offer in the new
millennium, how many will have anything worth watching?
To put it bluntly, are human beings up to handling all this
technological advance?

Any analysis of the present state of the world would have to
conclude that anxiety about its future is not mere human
cowardice in the face of the unknown, nor even an undue
alarmism. People who have no wish to speculate about the end
of the world, who may indeed think it improper to do so,
nevertheless have little difficulty in imagining a number of
different scenarios for earth-shaking, if not earth-destroying,
disaster. Some of our dangers as we approach the millennium
are new. We have made great strides in protecting ourselves
against the environment (though only the rich can enjoy such
protection), but for the first time in human history the
environment is seriously underprotected against us. We are
already beginning to see the ecological effects of the hugely
increased consumption of developed economies: global warming threatens low-lying countries with floods, the depletion of
the ozone layer leaves us vulnerable to the sun's radiation,
pollution destroys wild life, and sometimes human life. What
is worse is that we do not know precisely what damage we are
doing to the natural systems that sustain human life, and by
the time we do it may be too late for them to be restored. The

accumulation of nuclear waste which will remain potentially lethal for hundreds of years is an example of our readiness to incur bills which future generations will pay.

Nor is the more immediate threat of nuclear devastation unreal, whether by accident (witness Chernobyl) or by design. At the end of a century in which more people have been killed in war than any other, we may be grateful that the threat of superpower nuclear conflagration has disappeared with the ending of the Cold War; but nuclear weapons can never be uninvented, and nuclear proliferation seems unlikely to be contained. State governments perhaps can be supposed unwilling deliberately to make a first use of such weapons, but few people would feel equally confident about international terrorists. The last decade of the twentieth century has in any case exploded any idea that nuclear wars are the only wars to fear: genocide requires only machetes, or machine guns. The nationalism or tribalism that fuels such conflicts seems to be increasing since the end of the superpower stalemate that has dominated the second part of the century; and where ethnic and religious divides coincide, as they do in that most volatile of all world danger-points, the Middle East, the risks of war are compounded. In all this, international peace-keeping is in its infancy, and its development is not helped by the highly equivocal attitude to the United Nations of the world's remaining superpower.

Behind many of the world's conflicts lies competition for the ownership or control of scarce resources: land, oil, perhaps in the future water. It is above all in the state of the world economy that the roots of the threat to world peace can be found, as well as of the world's ecological distress. The threats are compounded by that economy's inbuilt injustice, which means not only a totally unacceptable inequality between rich and poor in what they are able to enjoy of the world's goods, but a system which offers the poor very little chance of achieving greater equality.

The increased consumption which has threatened the natural world has been concentrated in the hands of a small minority of the world's people, and the gap between rich and poor is widening. In 1960 the wealthiest 20% of the world's people were thirty times as rich as the poorest 20%; by 1997 the figure was seventy-four times.[1] The phenomenon occurs within as well as between countries, so that projections for the UK, for example, suggest that by 2010 the top 10% will be ten times as rich as the bottom 10%.[2] The 'trickle-down' theory, in other words, that wealth at the top leads in due course to increased prosperity at the bottom of the economic heap, has been comprehensively disproved in favour of the much older insight that 'unto him that hath shall be given'.

Much of this is due to the development of a global money market, dominated by transnational companies and commercial banks. This has embroiled the poorest two-thirds of the world in a debt which can never be repaid, but of which the servicing alone makes any economic development of the debtor countries impossible. Thanks to the Jubilee 2000 campaign, a millennial release from debt has entered the realm of practical politics. Entirely welcome though this is, debt relief leaves unaddressed the causes of inequality, and the pattern of economic activity will continue to mean that poor countries (and economic 'underclasses' in rich ones) are either exploited or, even more frighteningly, are simply ignored.

Perhaps even more sharply than in the sphere of world peace or of environmental issues, the world economic system raises the question of control. The major instruments of control in our world are national governments; but the economic system depends largely on money markets that cannot be regulated by national governments acting either alone or together. Those who trade in these markets are responsible to investors, and cannot be expected to act with other than narrowly sectional interest. Again, we may be taken where we do not want to go.

The sense of powerlessness which this sort of survey engenders is not equally felt everywhere, nor is the response to it uniform. Those for whom the present world system has 'worked' may well face the situation with relative optimism, even when the problems are taken with great seriousness. A recent North American treatment of today's 'global challenges', for example, has concluded that, given a sensible concentration of international attention on the problems which most need joint action, the situation is far from desperate.[3] But it is very noticeable that for this author poverty is a challenge because it cannot fight disease (and with increased world travel diseases can be communicated to other continents more easily), because it may lead to revolution, and because it leads to environmental degradation; it is not a challenge because the poor do not enjoy a decent quality of life. *That* problem is not taken with any seriousness – because it is not seen to be a problem. How people see the world depends on where they are looking from; and their response varies accordingly.

It would be far too simple, however, to suppose that the rich world in general feels optimistic about the possibility of controlling the world's future while the poor world does not. For one thing, as we have already hinted, the phrase 'rich world' is itself a serious oversimplification, because there is an increasing incidence of poverty within rich countries. What is more, people can be relatively well-off economically, and still have a sense of powerlessness. In the burglar-alarmed, high-fenced properties of comfortable Britain may there not be unacknowledged fears of rioting poor in the inner cities rampaging into the well-heeled suburbs, or even of untold millions sweeping across Europe from beyond the Mediterranean? Who can be sure that the system which has so far delivered the goods will not tomorrow see the stock market fall or the job disappear? How many can be confident that developing technology will not leave them way behind – and perhaps those in front will simply say 'get lost'? For the vast majority of the world's population, whether poor or comparatively rich, it is 'they' and not 'we' who are in control. And 'they' are either positively oppressive or at best not to be relied upon – do they know what they are doing, and do they care?

The two basic possible responses to fear are fight or flight.

Fighting requires an enemy, and our world is full of enemies. For the 'free' world the 'evil empire' of communism has collapsed,[4] but a vague 'Islamic threat' shows signs of taking its place; while much propaganda of this kind may be inspired by those who have an economic interest in a large defence industry, it is only effective propaganda because it speaks to people's fear. Many nationalist or ethnic conflicts are similarly fuelled by the tendency to project on to the nearest and most obvious 'other' the responsibility for ills which have much more complex causes. National or ethnic identity also gives a cause to fight for as well as an enemy to fight against, and is powerful too because it imparts a sense of knowing who you are and where you stand, thus addressing the uncertainty which is so large a part of fear. God is even better as a cause to fight for, and as a source of a confidence-building identity. Hence the 'hawkish' stance of much of the Christian fundamentalist right in the United States and the readiness of Islamic fundamentalism to resort to violence.

But fighting is not the only option, nor perhaps the one most often chosen. There is also 'flight'. This may be for the relatively advantaged a denial of the problems or a refusal to think about them: the present is at least moderately comfortable, and 'you die if you worry, you die if you don't'. For those for whom poverty, or war, or environmental disaster or degradation is a daily inescapable fact of life, thinking may seem a luxury: better to develop as much street wisdom as possible in coping with a basically hostile world, or perhaps just essential to get on with the physical work on which survival depends. There are too many immediate fears of personal or family distress or disaster to worry about the future of the world. Let the rich and comfortable do that – if only they would worry first about the injustices of its present. If the 'world view' behind such attitudes were to be articulated, it might be 'it is the will of God' or more simply that it's all down to luck, and if you're poor you're unlucky. For the poor, as for the rich, the 'flight' option means a shelving of the whole question.

But what is the Christian response? There is a Christian version of the optimistic view of our situation, though it usually looks the risk of disaster more steadily in the face. Where the secular response amounts to 'there is a great deal that is good about the way we are going, and if we get our act together we can sort out the problems', Christians may well be more conscious of the evils of our present, and less confident of human willingness to correct them; but they will be at one with the secular response in accepting fully that it lies with human beings to do the correcting. A global theologian who is willing to see the current world crisis as a 'revelation' in its exposure of our present danger and its hints towards a better alternative, nevertheless is anxious to emphasize that

> . . . what is revealed to us in the emerging situation has nothing to do with plans or predetermined scenarios. It has to do with new possibilities which are open for us to realize. The situation calls for responsibility, not infantile dependence.[5]

It lies with us, in other words, to do our best to put things right. We may certainly expect God's inspiration, guidance and succour for our efforts, because he wants all that is good for his creation, but in a fundamental sense he has put the world in our hands, and will not intervene to get us out of trouble, even if the trouble is catastrophic. The dangers we sense should accordingly lead us to the most urgent possible action for justice, peace and the care of the environment, in the hope, though by no means the certainty, that we shall avoid catastrophe and find a better way.

This is admirably courageous, but for many people it founders on the extreme unlikelihood of our most urgent possible action being enough. What chance has Traidcraft against transnational companies? What chance has our cycling to work got against car-owners' preferences for convenience and comfort? When will the rich ever invite the poor to the table rather than throw them crumbs? Since Jubilee 2000's at least partial success, no one can argue that political activism is *never* effective. But can it be expected to produce more than occasional results in a world crying out for amendment in a thousand different ways? 'What I do won't make any difference' is sometimes just an excuse, motivated by our desire to cling to the comfortable status quo; but it may also be quite a serious argument. If, as seems entirely possible, human sin means that human efforts to cure the world's ills are bound to fail, why make the attempt? If there is no conviction of God's being there to guarantee victory in the fight against the world's evil, then many Christians will refuse their call-up papers.

At the other end of the spectrum from the theology that says 'God has put the world in our hands, and he's going to leave it there' is Christian fundamentalism. This may, as we have suggested, be a home for very hawkish attitudes, but in essence it is the passive position of leaving everything in God's hands, and seeing the world's potential disasters (or more correctly its certain disasters) as all part of God's plan. This is of course only tolerable as a belief if something else is planned for Christians, and one can be sure of being among them; hence the millenarian beliefs in the 'rapture', the taking up of Christians to meet Christ at his second coming, after which the rest of the world may be left to judgment. But many Christians, much as they may long to believe that God is 'in control', cannot bring themselves to believe in a God who could consign untold millions so readily to damnation while saving the chosen few – or who meanwhile could *plan* for massacred children, for endless trails of refugees, for the poverty and starvation they see almost daily on their televisions. Yet if he does not plan these things, what possible meaning can be given to the idea of God's being in control? It is the old problem: either God is not good, or he is not God.

Many Christians simply retire defeated in the face of this dilemma. They cannot believe with 'world in our hands' Christians that human beings have any real hope of discharging the responsibility the optimists claim for them. But they cannot see what God is doing either. So, like many less believing people, they settle for something smaller and more immediate. World problems are too big, and God's role in them is too uncertain; let me get on with doing my best to be a Christian in my personal life, where I *can* see God at work.

This sort of 'privatized religion' may be just a selfish pre-occupation with the saving of one's own soul, but it is not necessarily anything of the kind. It can be a faithful loving of one's immediate neighbour which is very costly indeed. The trouble is that it leaves a great deal of life out. For today every-day living connects us as never before with the world at large. It is not just that we know about it through the media (whose coverage is in fact extremely selective and misleading), or that telecommunications can put us in touch with every country on earth. It is that every time we go into a supermarket we are taking part in the *world* economy. Our car exhausts contrib-ute to *global* warming. And we are beginning to realize that we even make some marginal difference to the way decisions get made in the world: technology is making it easier to mobilize and express public opinion, and we either take advantage of that or fail to do so. It is no longer possible to think that God's being the Saviour of the world means just that he is the Saviour of every individual in it, true and wonderful though that is. He is the Saviour of the world in all the complexity of its institutions and relationships, and we need to know what that might mean in practice, and how we might relate to it. Certainly, if we do not, we are left with no remedy for a quite rational fear about the state of the world and a quite justified sense of dis-ease about living so com-paratively comfortably in an unjust world. Blissful ignorance is no longer an option.

Is Revelation any help in our predicament? Many people would dismiss such an idea as scarcely worth examining. Has not Revelation been the happiest of hunting grounds for people interested only in saving their own souls while the rest of the world goes to blazes? Does it not encourage precisely the sort of 'it's all in God's plan' thinking which abdicates all human responsibility? It has to be admitted that the book has been read in this way. But if that is a true reading, how do we explain the book's long history of having inspired radical action? How can it be a book of 'comfort and protest', to quote the title of a commentary from the apartheid era of South Africa, for those on what has been called the 'underside of history'?[6] Is it not because many readers are inspired by Revelation's passionate conviction of God's victorious action, and *at the same time* hear its call to join in the action themselves? On this reading, a debilitating sense of powerlessness and a facile irresponsibility are equally excluded.

Revelation has some particular claims to the consideration of Christians living at the turn of the millennium. First is its global concern, more in tune, perhaps, than any other biblical book with our sense of living in one interconnected world. Thoroughly steeped in the Old Testament though it is, Revelation has none of the Old Testament's nationalism. Nor has it the primarily domestic feel of most of the New Testament epistles, in spite of being addressed to local congregations. It is concerned with the kingdom of the world becoming the kingdom of our Lord and of his Christ.

Second, with its amazing imagery, Revelation moves in the realm of the emotional, the imaginative, and the spiritual in a way that we are increasingly conscious of needing. We need language that expresses the enormity of our problems, and not just mind-numbingly boring statistical reports. We need solutions that are more than technical: we still rightly wonder at the advances of science, but we are abandoning our naive expectations of scientists and technocrats as saviours, and beginning to realize that world problems have to be addressed with the eyes of the heart as well as the calculations of the computer. In 1993 a Parliament of the World's Religions issued a 'Declaration Toward a Global Ethic'; our world predicament, they said, needs an ethic and an ethic needs a vision.[7] Revelation is essentially visionary.

Third, Revelation marvellously succeeds in connecting the church with the world. Revelation is a vision within a letter –

and the letter is to churches that for all the remoteness of their first-century context, are very recognizable: they are small, struggling, good in parts, but not altogether faithful, just like ours. The letters to the churches in chapters two and three are also quite ordinary in many ways (though rather more trenchant than we should dare to write). But then we find those letters are a sort of island in an immense ocean of visions of things in heaven and things on earth. And all the visions are there *for the sake of those little churches*. John is convinced that they have a crucial role to play in the world, and he passionately desires them to share his vision so that they may see that role and be moved to take it up. What could speak more directly to Western Christians today, who are so conscious of the enormous challenge of the world's predicament, and of the insignificance of the church?

For many Christians today Revelation is not at all a familiar book. If we are to examine its potential contribution to our understanding and responding to the challenges the world faces at the beginning of a new millennium, we need first to consider what is in the book, and to address the questions that may arise about it in the minds of today's readers. This is what Part One of this book is about. In Part Two we consider what Revelation's vision for us might be, and what it might mean for us to be faithful to that vision.

PART ONE

2

What is Revelation about?

The question 'what is Revelation about?' can be addressed on a number of different levels, but it is simplest to start with an account of the contents. Even that is not a simple matter: as one scholar has ruefully commented, 'there are almost as many outlines of the book as there are interpreters'.[1] So what follows is only one of many possible descriptions.

The book is an account of a series of visions seen by John;[2] he is told to write down what he sees, and send it to a group of churches to be read to the people there. Although the words 'and I saw' keep recurring in Revelation, so that at times the visions seem almost to be tumbling over each other, there are four basic vision groups, each of which begins with a reference to being 'in the Spirit', and has a distinctive theme and, some-times, location.[3] (There are links between the groups, and between groups three and four there is a substantial overlap, but it is probably worth oversimplifying a little for the sake of clarity.) The four groups cover the whole of the book, with the exception of a short introductory section (1.1–1.8) and a short conclusion (22.6–21); the shortness of these is in almost inverse proportion to their importance, but we shall leave them for the moment, and here concentrate on the visions.

The vision of the Lord of the churches and his word to them (1.9–3.22)

The first vision, which is very short, but crucial for the whole book, is a vision of Christ in glory; he appears to John as 'one

like the Son of Man' (1.13), and then dictates to him a series
of seven letters, each to a different church. These letters are
a mixture of praise and admonition, the latter sometimes
quite sharp; but even the most severely critical encourage
repentance, and each letter ends with a promise about the
ultimate reward of faithfulness.

Visions of the approaching end (4.1–16.21)

The second group of visions takes more than half the book,
and is where Revelation is at its most complex. The section
begins with Christ inviting John to come up to heaven, to see
'what must take place after this' (4.1). John sees first a scene
of heavenly worship of God, and then a scene where a sealed
scroll is given to a Lamb bearing the marks of slaughter; by
implication, it is this scroll which holds the secret of 'what
must take place'. The Lamb (who has, remarkably, been
announced beforehand as a Lion) is acknowledged as alone
being worthy to open the scroll, and earth and sea join heaven
in a chorus of praise to God and the Lamb together.

The scroll has seven seals, and the opening of them is the
first of three sequences of seven: seven seals opened, seven
trumpets blown, and seven bowls poured out. Each sequence
begins with a scene in heaven, and (except for the bowls
sequence) ends there; the sequences consist of a series of
disasters, which increase in intensity, so that by the end of
each series the world as we know it comes to an end, and the
way for the new creation is prepared.

It is not very clear why John has three sequences. On the one
hand, the events described seem to be increasingly terrible,
and this might suggest that John is predicting a three-part
programme of punishment before the end finally comes. There
are some formal details that fit with this idea, of which the
most obvious is that a quarter of the earth is affected by the
troubles in the seals sequence, and a third in the trumpet
sequence, while in the bowls sequence disaster is unlimited.
(This is the series of seven plagues, 'which are the last, for with

them the wrath of God is ended' (15.1).) Moreover, the nature
of the troubles is progressively 'out of this world' – whereas in
the seals sequence we see war, greatly inflated food prices,
famine and pestilence, the trumpets and bowls produce
falling stars and millions of cavalry troops riding lion-headed
and serpent-tailed horses, or seas and rivers turned into blood.
But other considerations tell against a 'programme for the
End' reading. One is the general point, developed later in this
chapter, that it is unlikely that John was in the business of
issuing predictions. Another comes from the text itself.
The seals sequence, though it begins with quite 'ordinary'
disasters, ends with language very reminiscent of the language
in the apocalyptic parts of the Gospels, which clearly suggests
that the 'End' has been reached by the end of the first
sequence.[4] It seems better, therefore, to think of the three
sequences as giving increasingly urgent warnings of the same
'events', with John wanting not to give information, but to
drive a point home ('what I tell you three times is true').

This question about the significance of the three sequences
is not the only, or indeed the most obvious, complication for
the reader of this central group of visions. More immediately
problematic is the fact that the sequences keep getting interrupted. The seals appear in chapter six and at the beginning of
chapter eight, but chapter seven is taken up with a vision of
the saints in heaven who are 'sealed' before the opening of the
seventh seal. The trumpets begin at 8.2, and do not finish until
11.19 (or perhaps 11.18); but half of chapters eight to eleven
are taken up with other visions. The bowls might be expected
to follow naturally straight after the trumpets – indeed John
seems to give his readers (or listeners) a nudge in this direction
by referring to the temple both at the end of the trumpet
sequence and at the beginning of the bowls one. Yet these two
sequences are separated by three chapters of very different
material.

The 'other material' is so substantial that it would be
unsatisfying to think of it simply in terms of digressions or
interludes, particularly because Revelation is so careful and

sophisticated in its construction that the reader is fully justified in supposing that everything is there for a purpose. Anticipating the results of discussion later in this chapter, we can say that some of the other material reflects John's concern with his own part, and his readers' part, in the world's story. Thus the first interlude which interrupts the seals sequence, chapter seven, gives an account of the 'sealing of the saints', which must be there to assure faithful Christians that they will be protected, not from suffering or death (which is to be expected), but from the destruction that is in store for the unrepentant.

The second block of other material is inserted within the framework of the sixth trumpet, and covers chapters ten and eleven. First John's own call to prophesy is described: in an account which very deliberately reminds the reader of Ezekiel's prophetic call, John is asked to eat a scroll, and then to perform a symbolic action.[5] This action, which is 'measuring the temple' (suggestive of the protection of God's people), is followed by a description of the 'two witnesses', who by their prophecy call people to repentance, though at the cost of their own death, which is followed by resurrection. These two witnesses are generally understood to represent the church, though other interpretations have been suggested, including one that sees the witnesses as standing for John himself.[6]

With the third section of other material, which comes between the trumpets and the bowls sequences, the pictures become increasingly bizarre, at least for modern readers, and we have to look for other explanations for their presence. In chapter twelve there is a heavenly confrontation between a woman who gives birth, and a great red dragon, from which the woman and her son escape; this is followed by war in heaven between the dragon (Satan) and Michael, culminating in Satan's fall from heaven and his pursuit of the woman and her children on earth.[7] In chapter thirteen the dragon is joined by first one and then a second beast, equally blasphemous, deceiving of the world and destructive of the saints. Chapter fourteen brings a change of scene, presenting John with the

Lamb accompanied by his heavenly army (who are the sealed 144,000 of chapter seven, where a military census has been taken of the twelve tribes). This is followed by visions anticipating the final judgment, which is described more fully in John's third major group of visions; here there are brief accounts of angels calling for acknowledgment of God, announcing Babylon's downfall, and warning of the punishment of those who worship the beast. This is followed by summary pictures of the grain and the wine harvest (probably standing respectively for those who are gathered to eternal bliss and those who are doomed to punishment);[8] the first harvest is gathered by one like the Son of Man (the description of Christ in the very first vision in the book), and the second is in the hands of an angel.

Apart from these final visions, this block of material serves chiefly to introduce more completely the dramatis personae of John's vision. For John, the ultimate reality is God and what God has done in Christ: God and the Lamb come first in his thinking and they have already appeared in chapters four and five. But equally real in human experience is the conflict in which John feels himself and his churches to be involved, and behind this conflict are spiritual realities on both sides: hence the pictures of war in heaven and on earth, and the 'satanic trinity', as it has sometimes been called, of dragon, sea beast and earth beast (sometimes also called the false prophet). Commentators have noted a number of detailed ways in which this trinity parodies the chief actors on the other side of the conflict – God, Christ and the Spirit, particularly conceived as the spirit of true prophecy.[9]

Visions of judgment (17.1–21.8 or 17.1–20.15)

John's third group of visions is of judgment. The first object of this judgment is Babylon. This great city is portrayed as a harlot who has corrupted the whole earth, and her downfall is greeted both with dismay and with rejoicing – dismay where people have colluded with her iniquity and rejoicing on the part of God's people who have obeyed his call to 'come out of her', and are now seen as ready to become the Lamb's bride. But behind Babylon are the spiritual powers at war with God, and so there are further scenes of judgment in which first the beast and the false prophet and their followers are destroyed by the Lamb and his army, and then Satan himself is thrown into the pit. This, however, is not Satan's final end, which is delayed until after the 'millennium' – which is the thousand-year period in which the saints rule with Christ on an earth free of the deceiver's wiles. Then Satan is released again, and after a final attempt on the city of the saints, he is thrown into the lake of fire and sulphur to join the beast and the false prophet in eternal torment. The final judgment scene is one where all the dead are judged individually; those whose names are not found in the Lamb's book of life are consigned to the fire, while those whose names are in the book live to share in the new creation, announced by God as the end of all his judgment.

Visions of the new creation (21.9–22.5 or 21.1–22.5)

The new creation is first described as 'a new heaven and a new earth' (21.1), and its mark is that there is no longer a division between the two. The picture is one of a holy city. In one sense it is still of earth, though it has come down from heaven, for it has walls, gates and a street. But these have to be described in heavenly language, for what distinguishes this city from any known to the old creation is that *it is a city in which God dwells*. And his presence, with that of the Lamb, makes the city the fulfilment of the whole natural and human creation.

When people have something to say, they normally take great care to explain at the beginning what they are about. This is certainly true of Revelation, which in the space of the first four verses not only gives a telegrammatic summary of the subject matter of the book, but offers no fewer than three clues about the sort of book it is (its literary genre, to use the technical term).

> The *revelation* of Jesus Christ, which God gave him to show his servants *what must soon take place*; he made it known by sending his angel to his servant John, who testified to the word of God and to the testimony of Jesus Christ, even to all that he saw. Blessed is the one who reads aloud the words of the *prophecy*, and blessed are those who hear and who keep what is written in it; for the time is near. *John to the seven churches that are in Asia* . . . (1.1–4a, emphases added).

The subject matter of the book ('what must soon take place') has been described above, although parts of it will be treated more fully in later chapters. Of the three indications of the *kind* of book Revelation is, it is the second and third that we now examine for the light they shed on its purpose; the fact that the book is a 'revelation' will be considered in the next chapter.

To begin at the end, with 'John to the seven churches that are in Asia': Revelation is a *letter*. The precise significance of the letter form is a matter of some debate, but its overall importance cannot be overstated: John has things that he most urgently wants to communicate to the churches. All the revelation and all the prophecy are for them. The very first vision, of Christ in glory, begins 'write in a book what you see and send it to the seven churches . . .' (1.11). To underline the fact that the visions are essentially to be communicated, they are preceded by actual letters, which Christ himself dictates. Though one of the fascinations of the book is that the letters are so ordinary and the visions so extraordinary, a careful reading reveals a number of verbal links between them. The word 'conquer', which is so clearly built into the formal structure of every letter, is a word used throughout the accounts of the eschatological battles and again in the picture of the new Jerusalem at the end of the book. In warning rather

than encouraging vein are the verbal parallels between the
'Jezebel' at Thyatira, who has refused to repent of her
immoral teaching, and the harlot Babylon described in
chapter seventeen: both will be destroyed and will bring
disaster on those who commit adultery with them. On the
other hand, the Philadelphians who are assured in the letter
that 'I will keep you from the hour of trial that is coming on
the whole world' (3.10) have the same assurance writ large in
the vision of the sealing of the saints in chapter seven:

> Do not damage the earth or the sea or the trees, until we
> have marked the servants of our God with a seal on their
> foreheads (7.3).

All this must mean that there is but one purpose served
equally by John the writer of prosaic (though forceful) letters
and John the visionary: that his churches should be encouraged in their Christian faithfulness and, as need be, warned to
repent of their failures to be faithful.

But are the churches in Revelation really 'John's' churches,
and what is his relation to them? The most natural explanation of the urgency of John's concern for the churches'
spiritual state might be thought to be the pastoral 'care for all
the churches' that is so obvious a motivation for the apostle
Paul,[10] and some of the details in the letters do certainly
suggest local knowledge. The best known of several examples
is the letter to Laodicea, which William Ramsay first showed
(from other evidence) to be a centre for banking, the woollen
industry and a medical school specializing in ophthalmics;[11]
John must surely know this when he writes:

> I counsel you to buy from me gold refined by fire so that you
> may be rich, and white robes to clothe you and to keep the
> shame of your nakedness from being seen; and salve to
> anoint your eyes so that you may see (3.18).

But other factors tell against a very personal pastoral link with the churches. The churches are too far-flung to be a natural pastoral unit, and there is no suggestion that they were founded by John as a travelling apostle. What is more, the fact that there are *seven* churches in such a number-conscious book cries out to be understood symbolically: seven being the number of completeness, John is writing for the whole church in the province of Asia (it cannot be that there are only in fact seven churches there, since we know from elsewhere in the New Testament that there were more). There is the suggestion that the seven churches were selected not for their importance (since Thyatira, for example, as far as we know was less important than places like Troas or Colossae which are not included) but because they were staging posts on a circular trade route through Asia – or even Christian postal centres![12] The supposition that Revelation has this inclusive character is confirmed by the fact that the major vision part of the book is clearly designed for all its readers, without distinction, and both the opening and closing sections assume that the whole book will be read by everyone.[13] It is worth noting, however, in the midst of all this inclusiveness that John chooses to retain in his book letters to individual Christian communities with their own particular characteristics. He knows how important the congregational life of the church is for forming Christian faithfulness.

We might perhaps imagine a bishop-figure writing a circular letter to such a large body of Christians – but even if we could be sure that this sort of hierarchical organization of the church existed when Revelation was written,[14] it is not easy, to say the least, to see the book as a typical episcopal utterance. What is more, John's normal tone, though certainly he is not afraid to speak authoritatively to people, is markedly unhierarchical: he is characteristically 'your brother' or a fellow-servant.[15] We come much closer to understanding the relationship between John and the people for whom he is writing if we attend to the second of his descriptions of the book, a *prophecy*.

It is easy for Christians today to think of prophets as

essentially Old Testament characters, but in fact New Testament Christians saw themselves as living in an age of prophetic revival, and prophets had an honoured place in the Christian community: Paul in his famous list of gifts within the body in his letter to the Corinthians places them second only to apostles.[16] Recent work on Revelation has shown how important the understanding of John as a Christian prophet is for the interpretation of the book as a whole.[17] In one sense the prophetic cast of the book is obvious. It is full of direct or indirect references to Old Testament prophecy. It is full of the prophetic desire for a faithful response to what the Spirit is saying to God's people: the urgency of this comes across in all the letters, and is unequivocally expressed at the beginning and ending of the book:

> Blessed is the one who reads aloud the words of the prophecy, and blessed are those who hear and who keep what is written in it; for the time is near (1.3).

> Blessed is the one who keeps the words of the prophecy of this book (22.7).

But quite sophisticated structural analysis of the book is required to see just how significant a category prophecy is.

Here we need to return to our outline of the contents of the book, where we described the sequences of seven as being interrupted by 'other material' (see above, pp. 19ff.). We could with as much justice say that between chapters four and eleven of the book, John's call to prophesy is interrupted by the sequences of seals and trumpets. The place to start in understanding this is chapter ten:

> Then the voice that I had heard from heaven spoke to me again, saying, 'Go, take the scroll that is open in the hand of the angel who is standing on the sea and on the land.' So I went to the angel and told him to give me the little scroll; and he said to me, 'Take it, and eat; it will be bitter to your

stomach, but sweet as honey in your mouth.' So I took the little scroll from the hand of the angel and ate it; it was sweet as honey in my mouth, but when I had eaten it, my stomach was made bitter. Then they said to me, 'You must prophesy again about many peoples and nations and languages and kings' (10.8–11).

There are two obvious echoes here. One, which we have already noted, is of the story of the call of the prophet Ezekiel, who is also commanded to eat a scroll so that he can go and speak the Lord's words to the Lord's people.[18] The other is from within the book of Revelation itself, as the reader is reminded of the scroll which in chapter five only the Lamb was found worthy to open. A convincing case has been made by Richard Bauckham, following earlier work by F. D. Mazzaferri, that the two scrolls are the same (though John has confused things for commentators by using the word 'little scroll' three out of four times in chapter ten); and that the movement from chapters four and five to chapters ten and eleven is all one story of the revelation of God's purpose, *a story of which John's activity as a prophet is itself a part.* On this reading of the book, the contents of the scroll are not revealed as the seals are opened one by one (because scrolls cannot be read until all their seals are undone);[19] nor are they revealed immediately after the opening of the seventh seal (since the silence in heaven that follows that opening is the beginning of an interlude in which the prayers of the saints are heard and answered by the judgment of the first six trumpet blasts). Instead the opening of the seals reaches its proper conclusion in 10.2, where the angel holds the little scroll *opened* in his hand, and then gives it to John. This reading gains strong support from the very first verse in the book, where the revelation is given by God to Jesus Christ, who 'made it known by sending his angel to his servant John'.

It is important here to remember Ezekiel throughout, and not just in the eating of the scroll. In Ezekiel, before hearing his call, the prophet has a 'throne-vision', with marked similarities to, though also considerable differences from, John's vision in chapter four.[20] The vision and the call are connected, not just in the sense that the prophet sees the God who is sending him and thus knows that he is God's authorized messenger, but because, in obeying his call, he becomes the instrument by which the heavenly vision is realized on earth, and God's sovereignty is established there. This obedience is worked out in the prophet's words and actions, and symbolized initially in the eating of the scroll.

In Revelation's case, it is not only a matter of establishing God's sovereignty, but of establishing it in the way determined by the Lamb, for John's call follows not only chapter four, but chapter five, in which it is shown that only the Lamb is worthy to open the seals of the scroll. We can think of the contents of this scroll, handed to John, as the whole story of the establishing of God's sovereignty on earth in the Lamb's way, a story which must, now that the Lamb has won his victory, take place 'soon' (1.1) – and it is a story whose very telling will be instrumental in its coming true. John's own prophecy will be part of this, but as we shall see below, the 'telling of the story' will also require the faithful acting out of it, and this will involve not only John, but all those who join with him in a Christian faithfulness that is prophetic. Hence the urgency of the book. Are the readers going to be actors who bring the story to God's conclusion, or merely those who put up an unavailing resistance to it?

How does John envisage this process of establishing the sovereignty of God? To summarize, and inevitably to over-simplify, the wrath of God, which is also described as the wrath of the Lamb, punishes and finally destroys those who oppose God, and destroys also those powers, earthly and spiritual, which have led them into that opposition. That makes way for the new heaven and the new earth, where the heavenly city is the place of perfect restoration and super-abundant creativity, as befits the place of God's dwelling. This process is set in motion by the slaughter of the Lamb, which paradoxically is seen as a victory; it is similarly remarkable that, in spite of all the violence and military language of Revelation, Christ himself uses no violence – his sword is the sword of his mouth.[21] The significance of this is examined in chapter four, which looks at the whole question of whether we can accept the picture of God and a Lamb who can apparently take in their stride so much destruction on the way to the heavenly city.

Interwoven with this great movement through the destruction of what is evil to the establishment of what is good is the story of what is happening to human beings. The majesty of God so sublimely expressed in chapter four would seem to be reason enough to require the obliteration of all that opposes God. But the appearance of the Lamb in chapter five shows that at the heart of God's purpose to establish his kingdom is his desire that human beings should share it with him. So the heavenly worshippers tell us as they celebrate the Lamb:

> You are worthy to take the scroll and to open its seals, for you were slaughtered and by your blood you ransomed for God saints from every tribe and language and people and nation; you have made them to be a kingdom and priests serving our God, and they will reign on earth (5.9–10).

God and the Lamb constantly appear side by side in Revelation, which means that human beings are constantly in God's heart. Judgment, accordingly, in Revelation, is not simply to clear evil out of the way, as it were; it is designed to produce repentance. It is not just that in the letters the churches are urged to repent to avoid judgment, though this is a constant feature of the letters.[22] When people *have* incurred judgment, repentance is looked for as a consequence (though not usually found).[23] It would be quite wrong, therefore, to assume a simple division in Revelation between the saints who have nothing to worry about and the sinners whom God has written off from the word go. And, as we shall see in chapter four, it is less clear than much of the blood and thunder of

Revelation would suggest that salvation is only for the elect few.

Nevertheless, it would be idle to pretend that the saints are not given priority attention by John. This is of course partly because he is writing for Christians – for people who have at least heard the call to be saints, however imperfectly they are obeying it. But it is more subtle than that. As we have already said (p. 28), faithful Christians have a place in the action of the final establishing of the kingdom. They are part of the Lamb's army; they resist, and suffer for resisting, the powers that resist God; what is more, as we shall see in chapter seven, they have a part in bringing others to repentance.[24] Their weapons are not the weapons of violence, but the Lamb's weapons of faithfulness to the truth and endurance. These are the qualities which the letters consistently praise, for John wants his people to see that they have the Lamb's power in them. The essence of being a saint is to 'follow the Lamb wherever he goes';[25] and it is to encourage that, above all, that John wants his people to understand, and be ready to take their part in, 'what must soon take place'.

3

Interpreting Revelation

It is one thing to approach Revelation with some idea of its contents and purpose, and quite another to start actually reading it. Even readers who are expecting something out of the ordinary may be somewhat nonplussed. Did John really see all that, and if so, what was his mental state? Or is it all in some sort of code, which we cannot be expected to understand? Perhaps some of the bewildering array of horsemen and locust cavalry, beast and dragon, fleeing mother and brazen harlot are purely imaginary, and others 'stand for' something? But even where they do stand for something, can we necessarily believe in the something they stand for? Our spiritual world doesn't seem to be as heavily populated as John's: what do we make of all these angels (even the churches have them) – or indeed of Satan? And what of the end of the world, which John saw coming 'soon'? Did he mean that literally, and if so, is not the whole book discredited by the fact that the world hasn't ended soon? All in all, is it really possible for today's reader to get anything from this book – except if they happen to enjoy a scary sci-fi read – or should it just be acknowledged to belong to an age that is past and gone?

Happily, there is some firm ground from which to start in responding to all these questions. Powerfully imaginative though the book is, it is also, as any commentary will point out, immensely carefully crafted. We are not, in other words, being confronted with the unprocessed outpourings of a crazy hermit cast off on a 'damned desolate island'.[1] And it may be that to understand the craftsman will leave us less at a loss in our appreciation of the artist.

John the craftsman inherits a written tradition in which he is deeply immersed. Part of the difficulty that today's readers have with Revelation is their lack of familiarity with the Old Testament, so that they do not pick up how much John is using it.[2] *How* he uses it is quite a complex matter, and we shall need to discuss some aspects of it in the next chapter; here it is important simply to note the degree of his indebtedness to his own scriptures. Sometimes there are parallels so close as to amount almost to direct quotation:

And the city has no need of sun or moon to shine on it, for the glory of God is its light, and its lamp is the Lamb. The nations will walk by its light, and the kings of the earth will bring their glory into it. Its gates will never be shut by day – and there will be no night there (Rev. 21.23–25).
Compare
Your gates shall always be open; day and night they shall not be shut, so that nations shall bring you their wealth, with their kings led in procession ... The sun shall no longer be your light by day, nor for brightness shall the moon give light to you by night; but the Lord will be your everlasting light, and your God will be your glory (Isa. 60.11,19).

Around the throne, and on each side of the throne, are four living creatures, full of eyes in front and behind: the first living creature like a lion, the second living creature like an ox, the third living creature with a face like a human face, and the fourth living creature like a flying eagle (Rev. 4.6b–7).
Compare
In the middle of it [it = a fiery cloud] was something like four living creatures ... As for the appearance of their faces: the four had the face of a human being, the face of a lion on the right side, the face of an ox on the left side, and the face of an eagle ... (Ezek. 1.5,10).

Then I turned to see . . . and . . . I saw one like the Son of Man, clothed with a long robe and with a golden sash across his chest . . . his eyes were like a flame of fire, his feet were like burnished bronze, refined as in a furnace, and his voice was like the sound of many waters (Rev. 1.12–15).

Compare

I looked up and saw a man clothed in linen, with a belt of gold from Uphaz around his waist. His body was like beryl, his face like lightning, his eyes like flaming torches, his arms and legs like the gleam of burnished bronze, and the sound of his words like the roar of a multitude (Dan. 10.5–6).

. . . Jesus Christ, the faithful witness, the firstborn of the dead, and the ruler of the kings of the earth (Rev. 1.5).

Compare

I will make him the firstborn, the highest of the kings of the earth (Ps. 89.27).

A few examples cannot, however, give an adequate idea of how *constantly* John quotes or alludes to the Old Testament. No fewer than 579 such allusions have been detected – which would give an average of 27 per chapter. Some are doubtless not deliberate quotations at all, but simply indicate how much the Old Testament is in John's bloodstream. That is indicated also by the fact that whole sections of the book sometimes appear to be using Old Testament models, more or less closely. There are the parallels with visionary experiences in the Old Testament, of which we have already noted two primary examples, but there is also marked use of themes from the Pentateuch (the first five books of the Bible), particularly the theme of the Exodus, God's rescuing of his people from slavery in Egypt and his bringing them to the promised land. Some of the writing in the trumpets and (especially) the bowls sequences, for instance, is very strongly reminiscent of the plagues God sent upon Egypt before the Israelites escaped. Nor is this just the use of appropriately colourful material by someone who knows his scriptures well.

A theological claim is being made: that the God who acted once to redeem his people and bring them to the promised land is doing the same again, in perfect form, in his action through Jesus Christ. In the same way the heavenly city, as we shall see in chapter five, in many ways resembles the garden of Eden: in Christ there is a new creation, but it is the old one made perfect, not the replacement of a reject. In all this John is thoroughly characteristic of the New Testament as a whole, which knows well that 'salvation is from the Jews'[3] in the sense that it is the God of Israel who is acting in Jesus Christ, but wants also to claim that in Christ God is doing 'a new thing'. The 'new thing' is not different in the sense of contradicting the old (for then God would have to be contradicting himself, which he cannot do); the newness is in the completeness with which God is now realizing his purpose.[4]

All this means that, whatever John may have seen on the island of Patmos, the eyes with which he looked and the mind which found the words to describe it were eyes and mind formed by his scriptures and by the early Christian community's developing tradition of interpreting them. At this point we need to take special note of a particular type of writing in the scriptures, which, though it has a relatively minor place there, is a substantial body of literature outside the scriptures. This is 'apocalyptic' writing (sometimes just called 'apocalyptic'), from the Greek word for 'revelation' (apocalupsis).[5] We deferred in chapter two the question of what John meant by calling his book a 'revelation', and this is an appropriate point at which to consider it.

'Apocalyptic' is nowadays used as quite a technical term, with corresponding disputes among commentators as to its precise definition. John probably did not mean to be particularly technical, but nevertheless he will have been self-consciously in a tradition of apocalyptic writing, even if, unfortunately, we cannot be sure just what he will have inherited, because we do not know what documents may have been lost, or the precise date of some of those that have survived. However, we can trace the main features of apocalyptic. Perhaps the primary one is the one directly implied by its name 'revelation': it is the showing of things that normally remain hidden to ordinary mortals. Very often the revelation is of what is to happen in the 'end time' (which makes it, to use Greek again, 'eschatological'); and among other elements typical of apocalyptic are the heavenly messengers who are used to show things, and sometimes to explain them, to the person having the vision.

It is questionable whether Revelation is quite as concerned with the 'end time' as it looks to be, but it most certainly has the primary apocalyptic quality of being self-consciously the revealing of something that people otherwise would not be able to see. We shall need to explore both these subjects in more detail later in the chapter. Meanwhile there are some other features of apocalyptic writing which Revelation displays on which it may be helpful to comment. One still faintly survives for us in the saying 'it's always darkest just before dawn', and, more clearly in the pantomime's last-but-one scene, where the hero and the villain have their final nail-biting fight: before God's Day dawns there is characteristically in apocalyptic a time of darkness and tribulation in which evil fights to its last gasp before its ultimate defeat. In Christian apocalyptic this time was some-times marked by the appearance of an 'Antichrist' figure.[6] What may look to us like the product of a fevered imagination is thus very often simply John using some of the stock images of his apocalyptic tradition.

Another mark of apocalyptic with which today's reader needs some help is its fascination with numbers. This means, for example, that certain numbers are symbolic. Seven is the number of completeness; four is the number of the earth, again with overtones of completeness (as in 'the four corners of the earth'). Sevens and fours abound in Revelation, often in quite sophisticated forms, so that it is quite self-consciously a 'global' book – it is telling the whole story of the whole earth. Three and a half (half of seven) is something essentially limited, instead of complete, whereas six is the number of imperfection (short of seven). This might appear to be the explanation for the famous 666 as the number of the beast, and no doubt the unmissable note of imperfection added to John's satisfaction in the number, but in fact its explanation is probably considerably more complicated. It is worth quoting the verse:

> This calls for wisdom: let anyone with understanding calculate the number of the beast, for it is the number of a person. Its number is six hundred and sixty-six (13.18).

Words can have a numerical value (arrived at by adding the numbers for each letter), and the fact is that 666 is the numerical value, in the Hebrew version, both for 'beast' and for 'Nero Caesar'. In a real mathematical sense, therefore, the emperor Nero '*is*' the beast. However, there are further possibilities. Six hundred and sixty-six is a 'doubly triangular' number – with a base number of eight.[7] That suggests a possible link with another passage in chapter seventeen, where there is a mysterious 'beast that was, and is not, and is about to ascend', later referred to as 'an eighth but it belongs to the seven, and it goes to perdition'; if eight has been established as Nero's number, then this is a reference to Nero, and the legend that he was expected to return after his death. In both passages wisdom is called for – and no wonder![8]

Every generation has people who enjoy complex mathematical puzzles of this kind, but on the whole they are a minority interest. We do not, fortunately, have to be in command of the more esoteric conventions of apocalyptic to get John's basic message, for a book which is a letter and a prophecy is primarily concerned to communicate, not to puzzle, and most of John's original readers will not have been mathematical geniuses either. But it is useful to be aware of the bare bones of the number symbolism, as no doubt they would have been, not so much because it adds to what the book is saying, but because it is a part of the book's artistry which it is good to appreciate.

The same applies to colour. The use of colour is effective for today's readers, especially if they think easily in colour, whether or not they appreciate its 'meaning', but in fact there is a conventional colour 'code' being used (though it is a highly problematic one for us in some respects): white is the colour of the divine world, on the whole contrasted with red, which is the dragon's (i.e. Satan's) colour, and stands for bloody power; scarlet and purple are the colours of debauchery; and black is the colour of disaster and distress, – though not of death, which is pale green. Clearly Revelation's use of white and black is a stumbling-block, in that it contributes to that insidious white/good – black/bad association which has helped to sustain the oppression of black people by white people. At a far less serious level, peers of the realm and bishops might not be too pleased with the associations of scarlet and purple. Or perhaps that is not entirely a joke – for one of Revelation's most marked characteristics, as we shall see, is to be radically critical of those who in the world's terms are powerful, and painting them in their 'true' colours is part of this (though it is highly doubtful whether John's targets today would be primarily the House of Lords, and episcopal dignitaries).[9]

This discussion of number and colour raises in a particular form a much more general, and very important, question about Revelation. Granted that we can learn first-century linguistic conventions about number and colour, can we transfer what is being talked *about* from John's time to ours? If 666 is Nero's number, for instance, how can it possibly mean anything to us that is relevant to our situation?

It has been said that 666 is the number of bar codes used in supermarkets, just as it has been said that John's picture of fire-breathing horses with lion's heads was the best he could do to describe a mobilized ballistic missile launcher.[10] It is easy to pour scorn on such interpretations as completely missing the point that John was writing for his own time, quite apart, in the latter case, from being far too literalistic. Today's readers, at least in the Western world, have mostly been brought up on a tradition of biblical scholarship which lays great stress on establishing the original meaning and the situation of the original readers, so far as that is possible, as a basis for going on to ask, in the words of one famous historical biblical critic, 'what must the truth . . . be [in our terms] if men who thought and spoke as they did put it like that?'.[11] But recently it has been recognized that the reader of a biblical text does have at least a significant part in determining what that text means. (The word 'text' here is used in the technical sense to mean any passage, long or short, from the book one is talking about; it has nothing to do with starting-points for sermons.) Try as we will to recognize and even ignore the 'prejudices' we have as white or black, poor or affluent, Catholic or Protestant, we cannot read a text as disembodied people with no viewpoint at all. Some people would go much further and say that it does not matter what the author was intending to say; the text stands on its own and is to be interpreted by the reader without any reference to a supposed 'original meaning'. We might well not want to go as far as that, thinking that 'original meaning' should at least be used as some sort of control on the range of readings of the text that can be accepted; but certainly the 'reader response' way of approaching the Bible helps us to understand why Revelation has been so powerful at different periods of Christian history. Where people have been conscious of very great evil oppressing or perhaps threatening to destroy them, its bizarrely extravagant language has spoken to and for them in a way that no more moderate language could do. But are we then to say that Babylon has at one time been the Roman empire, and then the Turkish infidel, and then the Roman Catholic church? And what is it today – the Pentagon, or the capital that Saddam Hussein is about to rebuild?

Perhaps the traditional 'historical critical' method of looking first at the book in its original setting can help us here. Because if we are to take the author's intention seriously at all, we must immediately realize that 'reader response' was precisely what he wanted to evoke. Commentators across the spectrum from the highly academic to the pastorally/ prophetically motivated have concluded that John wished to encourage his readers to a particular response to their political situation – and to do so by coming to view that situation from a certain standpoint (to have a vision of it, in other words).[12] But if there is a certain 'way of seeing' that John is trying to get his readers to adopt, cannot that way of seeing be used in all sorts of different historical settings? At this point we need to digress to examine rather more carefully what John's way of seeing might be.

We commented at the beginning of this chapter that John's spiritual world seems to be much more populated than ours, and we need now to examine why this is so, and whether we can possibly identify with John in this respect. It does not seem very likely. With all our increasing awareness that science may not solve all our problems, we still have a basically scientific world view, and things for us are most real if we can see them (seeing them in visions doesn't count). Guardian angels might seem like a nice idea, if rather twee, but not more; angels as messengers and spiritual guides are quite outside our experience; and the devil as dragon is frankly a pantomime figure, with the beasts and the rest of the improbable or impossible creatures that figure in Revelation finding their most natural place in horror movies.

But do horror movies not bear *some* relation to reality, and if they do, may they not reflect external realities as well as the dark places of people's psyches? Is it possible that 'good' spiritual beings, which figure much less substantially in fiction, also represent realities for which at present we simply have no words? In a remarkable trilogy of which the first volume appeared in 1984, Walter Wink has suggested a way of understanding the 'powers' that are so frequently mentioned in the New Testament, and so usually glossed over by ourselves, that makes them intelligible to today's Western readers while claiming a real existence for them.[13]

Working from a very thorough examination of the New Testament evidence for the powers, Wink suggests that this language offers a way of talking spiritually about human corporate and institutional experience, while retaining the closest possible connection between the spiritual and the material. With individuals we are accustomed to this: we understand that people are embodied, and cannot be or act spiritually independently of their bodies, but we are nevertheless at ease with describing them as persons in basically spiritual terms. Wink suggests a similar way of understanding and describing human groups and the institutional form they take, so that, for example, 'the "principalities and powers" are the inner or spiritual essence, or gestalt, of an institution or state or system'.[14] Similarly, in his discussion of the letters to the churches in Revelation, Wink says:

> . . . the fact that the angel is actually addressed suggests that it is more than a mere personification of the church, but the actual spirituality of the congregation as a single entity. The angel would then exist in, with, and under the material expressions of the church's life as its interiority. As the corporate personality or felt sense of the whole, the angel of the church would have no separate existence apart from the people. But the converse would be equally true: the people would have no unity apart from the angel. Angel and people are the inner and outer aspects of one and the same reality.[15]

This is spelling out the sort of thing we mean when we talk about a 'happy school', for example. We do not mean that everyone in it is happy all the time, but that *as a whole* it is happy. And this happiness is not a detached spiritual 'something', it is embodied and acted. It is the children's work put up on the walls, celebrating their achievements; it is the welcome notice and the flower arrangement in the entrance hall – the smile on the school's face; it is the 'ethos' which means that as a rule people are treated, without distinction, with kindness and respect. The happiness is real, and spiritual, but it is not independent of its outward forms.

This description of the spiritual 'inside' of something which is nevertheless essentially connected to a material 'outside' is a very powerful mental tool, because it allows us not only to speak of groups or institutions as a whole in spiritual terms, but also lets us use spiritual language for *aspects* of their life and behaviour, which may be quite transient. Wink uses the illustration of a football crowd:

A 'mob spirit' does not hover in the sky waiting to leap down on unruly crowds at a soccer match. It is the actual spirit constellated when the crowd reaches a certain critical flashpoint of excitement and frustration. It comes into existence in that moment, causes people to act in ways of which they would never have dreamed themselves capable, and then ceases to exist the moment the crowd disperses.[16]

This way of thinking is helpful for two reasons. In the first place, it allows us to recognize and express how *powerful* certain patterns of behaviour or institutional arrangements can be. Individuals in the football crowd would describe themselves as having been 'taken over'. Similarly it is not accidental that we talk about market 'forces': nobody chooses to close a factory and put people out of work, they feel compelled to do so. Our normal language tends to assume that when people do things, someone somewhere is in control; but this is not always true. Sometimes 'the powers' are in control. And to acknowledge this is not to abdicate responsibility ('it's not my fault – I just got taken over'); it is to realize how deadly it may be to put oneself in the hands of 'the powers'.

The second reason why it is helpful sometimes to concentrate on aspects of people's behaviour rather than people as whole individuals is this: it allows us to label behaviour of a certain kind or institutions in certain respects as demonic, or to use Revelation's other word, beastly, without labelling the people or institutions as demons or beasts. We can be serious about the evil that people do, in other words (and the more we recognize the uncontrollability of evil the more serious we shall be), without judging people in themselves to be evil. This is not to rule out the use of the nouns in extreme cases: a governmental regime, for example, may produce such consistently 'beastly' results that the name 'beast' is fully justified. But using the adjective to describe the behaviour is a much safer rule, because it helps us avoid the judgment of our fellow men and women as individuals. And if we can do that, we shall in fact be following the example of Revelation itself, which combines the most unequivocal condemnation of group behaviour and of institutions with a curious reluctance to pontificate on individuals' final destination. We discuss this further in chapter four.

Before we return to examine how this way of seeing might affect our reading of Revelation, we need to look at an even wider application of the principle of looking for the spiritual 'inside' of material realities. It is not just people, or groups, or institutions, or aspects of the behaviour of any of these that can be viewed in this way; it is also events. The most important real, earthly event in Revelation is the self-offering of Christ on the cross. But what readers see of this event they see in two visions that represent its spiritual reality: the Lamb standing as though it had been slaughtered, and Michael defeating the dragon and hurling him down from heaven. (In our much more boring abstract terms you might say that the standing Lamb represented goodness being unconquerable by evil, and that Michael's victory over Satan represented evil not being able to withstand goodness.) It is no accident that these are 'visions', for you could not possibly deduce the spiritual meanings by ordinary human reasoning, on the evidence of a man hanging on a cross or of small and uninfluential groups of his followers in danger of persecution by a hostile imperial power. But then that only goes to show how essential vision is, and why John is so urgent about sharing what he has seen.

The slaughtered Lamb and Michael's victory over Satan are seen in heaven, and that is highly significant. For heaven, in Revelation, is above all the place of spiritual reality. We need to set aside our preconceptions of heaven as the place of perfect happiness to which we hope to go when we die and earth is forgotten. Heaven is not even perfect in Revelation until it appears new at the End; Satan himself finds a place there until he is defeated by Michael and thrown out. And certainly heaven is not the place which really counts when earth doesn't, for, as we shall see in chapter five, Revelation is very much 'pro earth'. But heaven *is* the place where you can see the 'spiritual inside' of what is happening on earth, and of the people and institutions involved in what is happening – and where you see the God who 'was and is and is to come'.[17]

This understanding of John as presenting the spiritual realities that lie within earthly situations and events points us towards an answer to the question about how we can 'apply' Revelation to today's world. Spiritual realities are much less subject to change from one century than another than the outward forms within which they appear; indeed, perhaps one could argue that what is spiritual is in essence independent of time, because it is ultimately a matter of openness or opposition to the eternal God. Thus, for example, in every generation there are likely to be principalities and powers which display the same beast-like characteristics which John saw in the Roman empire, and we are not therefore wrong in looking for 'beasts', or at least for what is 'beast-like' in our own day. One might in fact say that we are being positively faithful to John in doing that, since his whole purpose in writing was to help people discern beastliness and resist it. Certainly, we need to resist the temptation to go overboard in seeing a modern equivalent for every detail, for if we take seriously the idea that 'material outsides' and 'spiritual insides' are essentially connected, then the spiritual inside of the Roman empire, which is what the beast was for John, will have the same uniqueness that the Roman empire had as a visible institution. Nevertheless, we should not be wrong to look for a strong family likeness (a common beastliness) among political powers which sustain themselves by military and economic dominance, oppressing people in the process, and which in doing so, whether deliberately or not, challenge the sovereignty of God. We do well, in other words, to allow ourselves to be 'envisioned' by Revelation as we look at today's world. But to attempt to transfer the vision lock, stock and barrel would not only lead to a good many bizarre and implausible identifications, it would almost certainly miss the point that Revelation above all requires a response from its readers. This brings us to the last part of our consideration about how Revelation is to be interpreted.

People who in their own day have supposed Revelation was 'really' talking about the defeat of whatever or whoever they saw as the primary source of evil in their world have normally taken the book very seriously as a prediction of the end time. Unless we are going to take an extreme view which says that it is the reader alone who gives meaning to the text and the author's intentions in writing it are irrelevant, we shall want to ask whether John thought he was making predictions. If he did, he was either wrong altogether, or at least wrong about the 'soon', and we shall need to ask how far that discredits his book. If he did not, then we shall be very reluctant to give too much credence to interpretations which see Revelation as 'coming true' in our day. (They are inherently improbable anyway. If Revelation can only 'really' mean one thing, then each successive interpretation means a lengthening list of people who have got it wrong in the past. But why should the latest interpretation be any more true than its predecessors?)

The most natural reading of Revelation would certainly be that when John said 'soon' he meant 'soon'. To live among people who seriously expect the world to end in their lifetime is so far removed from the experience of today's readers that we can scarcely believe that life like that is possible; yet it is clear from the New Testament that most first-generation Christians did believe just that, and it is not in one sense difficult to see why. If Christ was God's last word, the bringer-in of the kingdom, what was there to wait for? Christ at the end of his earthly life had returned to the glory of God and all that now remained was for him to manifest his glory and present the world to the Father. As time went on, and Christ did not return, New Testament writings reflect a coming to terms with that fact and a developing rationale for it; one of the most obvious adjustments can be seen in the fact that the author of Luke's Gospel described that book as being about what Jesus 'began to do and to teach', with a second volume, Acts, to continue the story into the age of the church, with no obvious end in sight. But it is unlikely that expectation of the End declined uniformly through the New Testament period and in all Christian communities. There would certainly have been an upsurge in expectation during the late part of the sixties of the first century with the Jewish war which ended in the sacking of Jerusalem by the Romans in 70 CE, and if we could be sure that Revelation was written then, we should certainly think that John's expectation of the End was to be taken at face value. In fact, though much of the material in the book appears to fit very well with that sort of date, scholars on the whole accept the statement of a late second-century writer that Revelation was written towards the end of the reign of the emperor Domitian (81–96 CE). This is a late enough date for many Christians to have abandoned their expectations of an imminent return by Christ, and it may well be that John's insistence that all that he has seen must take place soon is called forth by his people's growing reluctance to take the idea of the End with any real seriousness.

Perhaps we just cannot know how literally John expected the End to be 'soon'.[18] For whatever his actual expectations, it does not seem that he was primarily interested in making predictions. We have already suggested that the disaster sequences, for example, are artistically repeated warnings rather than a programme of expected events, and from much of the book it is difficult to extract any clear progression of events at all. The natural conclusion is that while John was passionately interested in *what* was going to happen, the *when* was a secondary question. The 'soon', in other words, functions more as a sign of urgency, expressed in temporal terms, than as a literal time-indication. ('The end is near' might be thought of as the temporal equivalent of the spatial 'heaven is very close'.) This sort of reading is wholly consistent with the prophetic urgency we have already described. It is the *present* faithfulness of his people in which John is really interested. The vision of the future is to inspire them to that: what is important is that they act now in the light of the End – whenever it may be.

If that is so, questions about whether John was right or wrong about the timing of the End become simply irrelevant, and a distraction from hearing the message that we should be living *now* in the light of the ultimate spiritual realities that he has seen. It is if John is mistaken about those realities that Revelation is in real trouble as a book for today's Christians. To that subject we turn in the next chapter.

4

Can we Accept Revelation?

Is Revelation really Christian? Granted, it is a lively, not to say mind-blowing, read. Granted, there is a serious and urgent prophetic concern for God's will to be done by God's people in God's world. Granted, the people who decided what should be in the Bible thought it should be included (just about).[1] But where is the love and mercy of God amidst so much violence and destruction? Where is the reconciliation that Christ died to bring amidst so uncompromising a conflict between the armies of good and evil? How can we sing for joy as people are thrown into the lake of fire? And even if it were Christian, is it credible? God has not shown himself to be a great zapper of people so far – why should he suddenly start? Reluctant as we may be to say this of a book in the Bible, has John just got it wrong?

Let us start with the picture of God with which Revelation presents us. Our assessment of how Christian that is will depend more than anything else on what we think John has done with the traditions he has inherited from the Old Testament and from apocalyptic writing. How far, to use the title of a ground-breaking book in the study of Revelation, has there been a 'Rebirth of Images', so that what looks at first sight to be merciless and unforgiving is not really so?[2] Does the central image of the slaughtered Lamb, which is dramatically *un*warlike, mean that the descriptions that look so violent are not violent really, but are claiming that Christ's truth-telling and patient endurance and suffering until death will in the end be as irresistible as (indeed, more irresistible than) all the violence in the world? G. B. Caird's comment on Rev. 5.5–6, where John *hears* of the Lion of Judah, and *sees* the slaughtered Lamb, expresses this view well:

> Throughout the welter of Old Testament images in the chapters that follow, almost without exception the only title for Christ is the Lamb, and this title is meant to control and interpret all the rest of the symbolism. It is almost as if John were saying to us . . . 'Wherever the Old Testament says "Lion", read "Lamb".' Wherever the Old Testament speaks of the victory of the Messiah or the overthrow of the enemies of God, we are to remember that the gospel recognizes no other way of achieving these ends than the way of the Cross.[3]

This sort of reading of the text certainly greatly helps the Christian reader, but is it justifiable?

There are strong reasons for saying yes to that question. For one thing John obviously means the Lamb vision to be taken with immense seriousness: its importance could scarcely be more clearly signalled in the way it is presented. Together with the vision of the sovereign creator in chapter four it is obviously intended to be definitive for all that follows, and the fact that chapters four and five are placed together in this way surely means that God and the Lamb are to be understood in terms of each other. This very close association of God and the Lamb is repeated throughout the book: time after time God and the Lamb appear together as the object of people's worship (or occasionally terror). What is more, the stark presentation in chapter five of the Lamb standing as if slaughtered, with the double assault on the reader of a Lamb when a Lion had been indicated and the impossibility of a slaughtered Lamb standing, has to be a deliberate underlining by John of the sacrifice of Christ: it is precisely this *suffering* of violence (rather than its imposition) that is being shown to be at the heart of God and of his purpose.

For all that, it is not clear that the vision of the Lamb can bear quite the weight of 'Christianizing' the book as a whole that we might wish. There is a good deal of material which it will not cover. True, Christ (and Christians with him) may fight and conquer using only the weapons of faithful witness and suffering; indeed, the imagery used of Christ and the requirements John lays upon the churches very positively support this interpretation. But in some of the most violent passages of the book, where the judgments of God on a sinful and unrepentant earth are described, no such redefinition is possible; the whole point is that there should be destruction. And even where the redefinition of Old Testament language is possible, how far has it actually happened? Has the 'Lamb' image really made all the 'conquering' and 'ruling' into something done only by the power of love, or are we being presented with a Lamb who for all the centrality of his sacrifice also has a ferocious side? It is remarkable that John quotes from none of the Old Testament passages which might suggest a more Lamb-like Christ and a less violent way of establishing his reign; instead we are unequivocally presented with the Messiah of Jewish expectation, who will rule with a rod of iron. Are we not in fact being asked to see the Lamb in terms of the Lion quite as much as the other way round?

Perhaps part of the difficulty lies in an ambivalence in John himself. Clearly he is committed to the way of patient endurance, and suffering if need be, for the followers of Christ (though it is not as clear as has sometimes been supposed that either he or those to whom he was writing were suffering acutely).[4] Clearly also he does not see the suffering of Christ simply as a great wrong crying out for vengeance; rather the saving significance of Christ's death is greatly to be celebrated, as we shall see in chapter five. The worship of the slaughtered Lamb is central to the book, and doubtless also a reality in John's own experience. And yet John displays no discomfort at all at the violence for which the God of the Lamb is ultimately responsible, indeed occasionally he positively exults in it:

And I heard the angel of the waters say, 'You are just, O
Holy One, who are and were, for you have judged these
things; because they shed the blood of saints and prophets,
you have given them blood to drink. It is what they
deserve!' (16.5–6).

Not many Christian readers today will feel that that is how
they have learned Christ, though they may well reflect that to
be Christian is not to be immune to such feelings, and that
where they exist it is not healthy simply to pretend that they
do not. It is also to be appreciated that John for all his passion
is rigorous about vengeance being in God's hands and not
human ones: you may rejoice when God does something to
punish the wicked, but you have to wait for him to do so when
he chooses. But at the end of the day, most readers will be conscious of an uncomfortable disparity between Christ the slaughtered Lamb and the tone of much of the rest of the book.

Given this ambivalence, the reader has a large role in
deciding where John really stands. John has given his readers
one central image of the slaughtered Lamb to set against a
great many extremely un-Lamb-like quotations from the Old
Testament, which carry a cumulative resonance of warlike-
ness completely at variance with the meekness of sacrifice.
Inevitably it is the reader who has to decide which image/set of
images is the more powerful, and this is why scholarly opinion
is so divided about Revelation, all the way from seeing it as
deeply Christian, with a complete 'baptism' of Old Testament
images by the Lamb on the cross, to an essentially Jewish
work, with a Lamb which is very little different from the
lambs typical of apocalyptic writings, which are basically
destructive and avenging creatures.[5]

To some extent the reader's decision will depend on the
interpretation of particular passages. An important example
comes just before the judgment visions:

So the angel swung his sickle over the earth and gathered
the vintage of the earth, and he threw it into the great wine

press of the wrath of God. And the wine press was trodden outside the city, and blood flowed from the wine press, as high as a horse's bridle, for a distance of about two hundred miles (14.19–20).

This echoes more than one traditional description of the destruction of sinners.[6] But how can it not also suggest to Christian ears the shedding, outside the city, of the blood in which sinners may wash their robes? It is difficult to hear this echo of the crucifixion and not suppose that John is setting against the traditional picture of the destruction of the wicked the Christian answer to it. If he is, the Lamb must surely have the last word. And yet very clearly John also believes in some real sense in the destruction of the wicked. Before trying to account for this, we need to confront the issue of Revelation's idea of judgment in its most problematic form: how can John describe the worst and most lurid of disasters as the wrath of God, and of the Lamb?

One response to this question is simply to deny that God is an angry, punishing God, at least in any obvious or direct sense. God's 'anger' does not impose disaster, but rather allows it, because God will not interfere with human beings' free will. 'Wrath', in other words, is what God will not stop us doing to ourselves. This view is lent a good deal of support by an examination of the passages in Revelation where the words for 'wrath' and 'fierce anger' are actually used. The classic study here, A. T. Hanson's *The Wrath of the Lamb*, pointed out how many of these passages refer to historical events, with historical causes, and concluded that the wrath of God was 'the working out in history of the consequences of men's sins'.[7]

There are certainly parts of Revelation where this view is very convincing. At the beginning of the seals sequence of disasters, for example, the second horseman 'was permitted to take peace from the earth, so that people would slaughter one another', and the appearance of the third horseman is the signal for the cry, 'a quart of wheat for a day's pay, and three quarts of barley for a day's pay ...' (6.4,6). We have no difficulty at all in seeing human causes for these troubles. Similarly, when the fall of Babylon the whore (Rome, for John) is predicted, though the language is bizarre 'spiritual inside' language, human agents are clearly involved working through historical events:

> And the ten horns that you saw, they and the beast will hate the whore; they will make her desolate and naked; they will devour her flesh and burn her up with fire. For God has put it into their hearts to carry out his purpose by agreeing to give their kingdom to the beast, until the words of God will be fulfilled (17.16–17).

The Roman empire, in our prosaic words, has the seeds of its own destruction within it.

But the second part of that passage raises a problem. If 'God has put it into their hearts to carry out his purpose', is this not God pulling the strings in a way that makes nonsense of human free will? In that case God is the cause of all the 'wrath' and 'fierce anger' just as much as if we take Revelation at its face value. And in any case, is there not a good deal of disaster that we cannot plausibly ascribe to human beings? It is noticeable that as the 'sevens' sequences progress, what God 'allows' becomes more and more outside human agency, and in several cases it gives way to what God simply does.[8] The point at which the supremely difficult (for most Christians today) 'wrath of the Lamb' comes is at the extreme 'end-time' part of the seals sequence, where, after earthquake and vanishing sky, the whole of humanity, from king to slave, cries out to mountains and rocks:

> 'Fall on us and hide us from the face of the one seated on the throne and from the wrath of the Lamb, for the great day of their wrath has come, and who is able to stand?' (6.16–17).

This cannot be, can it, what human beings have done to themselves?

We have to face squarely at this point the differences between John and ourselves. Most obviously, this end-time language was a familiar part of his tradition, whereas we have given the idea of the end of the world so wide a berth for so long that any language about it is likely to be very difficult for us. More importantly, John is far less reluctant than many of today's Christians are to think in terms of God's punishing people. It is not only, or indeed primarily, that he is out for retribution, though sometimes that certainly appears to be his dominant desire. He also has a clear sense of punishment, and the threat of punishment, as discipline: there is a great deal of 'repent, or else I will . . .' in the letters to the churches, and when judgments are visited on people elsewhere in the book, there is on a number of occasions the implied intention to bring them to repentance.[9] But even more fundamental for John than punishment as discipline is punishment as the establishment of God's righteousness: God in the end cannot tolerate evil, and the offence of it has to be removed – if necessary with the offender as well. Can this be reconciled with the Lamb who utterly disables evil by absorbing it? Here is Revelation's basic ambiguity again.

Before attempting to respond to that ambiguity, we have to look at a final area of difference between John and many (though by no means all) of today's Christians, and it is perhaps more important than any other. This is the question about how God acts in our world. John has no difficulty with what we would today call an 'interventionist' God, a God, who because he is sovereign over what he has made, can intervene to do whatever he chooses whenever he chooses, whether that is to put certain ideas or desires into people's minds and hearts at given moments in history, or to put things right at the end of time by a massive sweeping away of all that has spoiled creation. Many of John's readers today, on the other hand, cannot believe that God intervenes in that sort of way; it seems to make the idea of human freedom quite unreal, not to mention making God appear arbitrary and unjust. (Why does he choose to intervene, for example, as we would have to say

he does, to cure one person and not another, when they are
equally good, and equally prayed for?) Yet people do not want
to say either that God does nothing in the world; such an idea
would make nonsense of the entire Christian story of Jesus
and the Spirit, and equal nonsense of the prayer 'Thy will be
done'. Is there another way of understanding how God acts in
the world, and would Revelation make sense understood in
that way?

Modern theological thinking offers a possible answer.
Instead of God's acting in a series of individual interventions,
the whole process of human history is seen as one creating/
saving act of God; within this history human beings have
genuine freedom of action, rather as if God were the author of
a drama in which the actors were given their characters and
their general setting, but were then allowed to improvise their
parts.[10] This is light years away from Revelation's world view
in one sense, and yet it might fit surprisingly well with a
reading of Revelation which stresses the dominance of the
vision of the slaughtered Lamb. The victory of the Lamb
would then be understood as the love of God in the crucified
Christ being so powerful that ultimately it brings all the actors
in the drama to the conclusion the author intended. This
might sound as if people are, after all, being compelled, but it
is a paradoxical truth that, where love is, people speak of
being compelled where they are in fact acting most willingly.

Where would 'wrath' figure in such an understanding? It
would be part of the 'general setting' for the drama, 'the way
things are in the world'. 'Wrath' stands for the twin facts
that evil done has evil consequences and that there is an inner
rottenness about evil that ultimately leads to its collapse (this
is the inner truth of the eschatological, or end-time, wrath in
Revelation, an inner truth which can sometimes be observed
before the end, in the collapse of evil political systems, for
example). The love of the Lamb is not a sentimental veiling of
these facts, far less an attempt to alter them, for love can be
very hard sometimes (though human beings, being ignorant
and often judgmental, probably do well to embark on 'hard'

love only with great reserve). But the love of the Lamb stands eternally to receive those whom wrath or the fear of wrath has brought to repentance, and to pay the price of endurance until evil has exhausted or destroyed itself.

In all these attempts to interpret Revelation, we must acknowledge that we are finding today's solutions to today's problems. Just as John would have found incomprehensible our difficulty with the idea of an interventionist God, so he would not have been nearly as conscious as we are of the dissonance between the slaughtered Lamb and the destruction of the wicked. This is partly because he sees the destruction of the wicked in far less individualist terms than we do: while we are asking what is happening to all the people suffering plague and thunderbolt, he is most often thinking of the destruction of 'the wicked' en bloc, as it were (or, as we might put it, of wickedness); for John what happens to individuals in the end is settled somewhere quite other, as we shall see later on in this chapter, and he is far more reserved about it. We need also to remember that John's received scriptures are the Old Testament, in which the wrath of God is a standard idea, whereas we are at the other end of nearly two thousand years of evaluating the Old Testament in the light of the crucified Christ. And that suggests what is in the end probably the fundamental explanation of the ambiguities in Revelation and the dissonance between the Lamb vision and other parts of the book: that John has not fully integrated that vision in all its spiritual depth with other things that he thinks and feels.

That is not remarkable. It is a universal part of Christian experience that there are parts of us that have not yet been reached by the best that we believe, and that is true not only of our behaviour (we don't live up to our beliefs) but of what we think (we are inconsistent). John is very much 'John our brother' in that respect. We do not have patronizingly to excuse him for being a man of his time, though we do well to recognize the ways of thinking that belong to his time and not ours, and translate some of what he says into our language.

What we do have to do is to recognize his humanity, and be grateful for what *is* remarkable about Revelation: that the vision of the Lamb retains its central place in spite of being so much at variance with some of the rest of the book. We may accordingly take the central image of the slaughtered Lamb as *our* controlling image without supposing that it was wholly controlling for John.

But may we? Is it for us to decide that writers are being inconsistent, so that we choose which bit is more Christian? Are we justified in reinterpreting what the Bible is saying until it says something we can believe? Even to put the questions rings loud warning bells. Who are we to pick and choose, and alter the Bible?

Clearly the greatest humility is in place here. We are not very clever, and we are deeply self-interested; left to ourselves to decide what the Bible is 'really' saying, we shall probably get it badly wrong. We therefore need as many checks as possible from our fellow-Christians in our reading of the Bible, as much respect for traditional understandings, and as many prayers as possible for the guidance of the Holy Spirit (who is surely as much to be invoked in the reading of scripture as trusted to have inspired the writing of it). But with due consciousness of our own human fallibility as readers of the Bible, we must accept that we have also to take into account the humanity of its writers. Like the church the Bible is both human and holy, and it is a mistake to forget either the holiness or the humanity. It is characteristic of our risk-taking God that he puts himself into human hands, and speaks through and to imperfect people who are limited by their own time and place and experience. Not only does this mean that readers of our time and place are bound to translate writing from John's time and place into our own terms. It also means that John could sometimes have been inconsistent, or even plain wrong, in what he wrote. In the last resort today's readers have to judge for themselves whether they think he was.[11] But in making that judgment they would do well to learn from a book which is so aware of the danger of hiding from unpalatable truths: the Word of God is very often not what one would like to think.

'How Christian is it?' has to be the first problem question about Revelation. But there are others, and of very nearly equal importance. For example, even if we resolve the 'Christian' question in Revelation's favour by placing the central emphasis on a God who wins his victories essentially through the Lamb, are we right in the first place to think of the whole of life as a battle? Certainly Revelation seems to do so: there is warfare from beginning to end. There is the repeated 'he who conquers' in the seven letters to the churches at the beginning of the book, its centrepiece is the war in heaven between Michael and the dragon, and the drama ends with Satan's final losing battle in chapter twenty; not till the new world of the last two chapters are we free of this war between good and evil as a dominant category for understanding life. True as this may be to many Christians' experience of conflict, is it really the best picture of what life is about?

There is both a theoretical and a practical aspect to this question. Theoretically, the 'dualism' of a world divided between good and evil is suspect, and perhaps especially so when it is personified in a battle between God and the devil. Are not the mysteries of existence better understood as a unity (perhaps 'envisaged' is better than 'understood'), as one connected whole whose connectedness it is our business to seek after and our hope one day to see? And anyway, if everything is divided between good and evil, how can one be sure that good will win (many of the signs around us are not at all promising)? This leads to the practical question. In a battle of this kind, especially if there is any lurking uncertainty about its outcome, are we not forced into seeing human beings as essentially divided, by the most dangerous division of all, into 'goodies' and 'baddies' – with the inevitable temptation for the goodies to do bad things in order to win? Our previous discussion has almost all been about whether God is less than good in his defeat of evil; and if there are doubts about God, what chance have human beings? Are we not on the way to all sorts of violence against 'evil' people, or at least either some very unpleasant attempts to force them to be good or a smug sanctimoniousness that sees them go to hell without a tremor?

When we examine the theoretical question, we may be surprised at finding a different problem from the one we expected. So far from there being a battle whose issue is in doubt to the end, it almost looks as if God has stage-managed the whole thing. We have already noted the (to us) disturbing degree to which God pulls the strings for human beings; but the same looks to be true for Satan as well. It is the end of the story which makes this clearest: Satan can only gather his forces for the final battle in chapter twenty because he has been set free from his millennial prison (by whom if not by God?), and he and they are consumed in a moment by fire from heaven. But this only makes overt what we would suspect from seeing how Satan's chief agents are described in chapter thirteen: the beast is '*allowed* to exercise authority for forty-two months' and the second beast similarly deceives the earth's inhabitants 'by the signs that it is *allowed* to perform on behalf of the (first) beast'. So is it all a charade, a mock battle after all? If so, what is God playing at?

John would no doubt find that question little short of blasphemous, though the Old Testament in several places comes close to asking it,[12] and it is an inescapable question for anyone today wrestling with the problem of evil. For in the end, there seem to be only two ways to go – either God is not responsible for evil, and so cannot be relied upon to defeat it, or he is responsible for it and has to answer for all the pain and misery it causes on its way to final defeat. In the shorthand we used in chapter one, either God is not God, or he is not good.

Perhaps the only way out of this impasse is to look at the people puzzling over the questions. In a book called *Theology and the Problem of Evil*, Kenneth Surin argues that it is a fundamental mistake to ask about the evil in the world as if we were somewhere outside the world looking in (or on).[13] If we do so, we make two complementary errors: we make God too small – as if he were an object we could look at – and we fail to take account of our own being tied up with the world and the evil within it. Surin does not mention Revelation, but he points out that neither the early Christian Fathers on the one hand nor liberation theologians today on the other would countenance such a detached response to the problem of evil. Both are wholly in tune in this with Revelation, which is essentially about responding to evil from an *inside*-the-world position. John is issuing a call to arms in the fight against evil, and offering an assurance of victory, and thus vindication, for those who suffer innocently in the process; he would have little patience with 'armchair' questions about evil.

That does not mean we must abandon the traditional questions of theodicy, as it is called (literally 'God's justice' questions, raised by the existence of evil). Anyone who suffers, or identifies with sufferers, must ask 'why' in the sense of 'how can I make sense of this'? But the biblical answer to this is in terms of our relationship with God, not of an independent judgment about how he works. In the great Old Testament wrestling with the problem of evil and suffering, the book of Job, Job is genuinely answered in the end by being brought to accept that he cannot understand his infinite God. Similarly Revelation invites both saints and sufferers from judgment to make sense of their experience of evil in terms of identification with the suffering Lamb or resistance to him. We are not biblical people, and we cannot undo our intellectual history, which includes the Enlightenment discovery of how much you can do by experimenting on the world from 'outside' and seeing how it works,[14] so we shall no doubt go on asking, 'but why has God made the world like that?' But even we are beginning to realize that there is no such thing as a completely detached scientific observer. So perhaps our ears are opening to the fundamental reminder of Revelation's first 'throne vision' of God: all our questions have to take place *within our engagement with the ultimate* 'You [who] created all things, and by your will they existed and were created' (4.11). We are simply unable to pass independent judgment on the creation.

If we follow Revelation's way of thinking, then essentially we are going for the 'let God be God' option, and taking the goodness of God on trust, despite appearances to the contrary. We shall believe that God's goodness will be displayed in his *ultimate* defeat of evil (as it was displayed to the eyes of faith in the Lamb's victorious encounter with evil on the cross); and then, instead of constantly asking why his goodness allows so much present evil, we shall concentrate on the fight against it to which he calls us. But, granted that what is required of us is faithful response to the world from within it rather than pseudo-detached armchair questioning about it, is faithfulness really meant to be so relentlessly confrontational as Revelation would have us believe? Or is there perhaps a problem with Revelation's conception of the majestic, sovereign God above the world and sitting in judgment upon it, so 'other' or, to use the theological term, so 'transcendent' a God?

This is perhaps the point at which to note the difficulties which many feminist readers have had with Revelation, though by no means all of these have been about its confrontational tone or its ideas of God's sovereignty and transcendence. Revelation has been seen as more fundamentally misogynist in its pictures of women, which are sharply polarized: on the one hand is the idealized pure (the heavenly city as bride at the end of the book, or, slightly less obviously, the woman in chapter twelve) and on the other the whore (Jezebel at Thyatira in the letters and most notably Babylon in the visions, coming to her ghastly end).[15] Both are seen as male fantasy and attempt to control. It is easy, and in one sense correct, to defend much of this writing in terms of the Old Testament imagery which John inherits; and the Old Testament background is certainly the explanation for the offensive verse at 14.4, where the Lamb's army are those 'who have not defiled themselves with women, for they are virgins'. This refers to the prohibition of sexual intercourse before military duty, as well as using the general Old Testament imagery of unchastity meaning unfaithfulness to God.[16] But clearly there is a substantial element of misogyny in this tradition, which John has, to say the least, unquestioningly taken over.[17]

But feminist theologians have also been concerned about the dualism of a world view where there is so sharp and all-embracing a division between good and evil. The more typical feminist view would be to see life as an 'interweaving of good and evil, of passion, pain and celebration'.[18] And a sovereign and transcendent God is suspect as a remote and masculine figure, from whom control by violence is only to be expected. Nor are feminists alone in making this sort of objection. In an interesting essay, Johan Galtung has suggested that 'hard religion' of this kind leads to all sorts of human lording it over others (humanity over nature, men over women, some ethnic groups over others).[19] It would be very unlikely on his view that the way to a new earth would be one of continual 'conquering'. For even if to conquer is to resist passively rather than to use violence, is there not a destructiveness of thought about it that will eventually emerge one way or another? Does not Revelation itself show vengefulness breaking out, even if on the whole the objects of it are systems and not individuals? And even if the destructiveness were fully suppressed, could it really be of God?

There is much that is persuasive about this way of thinking, though in part it is unfair as a criticism of Revelation itself. The meaning of transcendence is that God is beyond us, and this applies to his sovereignty as much as to anything else about him. Earthly authority which tries to imitate God is in fact blasphemous, and it is clear that one of Revelation's key concerns to establish this.[20] Nevertheless, any honest review of Christian history has to acknowledge with shame what Christians have done in the name of their *Almighty* God, both to other people and, as God's vice-regents, to the non-human creation.

But does that mean that we have altogether to rule out the 'hard religion' which fights and conquers? How else should we respond to Auschwitz and Hiroshima, to the massacres

and murderous dictatorships that fifty years later still deface
our world, to the systematic exploitation and discrimination
that are daily life for millions? Must we not precisely *fight*
these things? And is it not helpful to have the sort of
fighting imagery which Revelation provides to alert us to the
evil and motivate us to the fight? Evil knows, after all, what
it can gain from speaking of a 'final solution' or of 'collateral
damage'; do we not need language that speaks of evil's
enormity?

But the dangers of 'hard religion' are real, and there are
two important rules that have to be followed if they are to be
avoided. First, fighting evil should not mean that its perpet-
rators are thought of, or treated, as enemies; a long and
honourable Christian tradition of passive resistance, not least
on the part of black Christians in North America and South
Africa, has shown us that the temptation to do so can be
resisted. Second, judging situations as evil, and far more so
people, has to be done with great restraint. All-out war is
simply an inappropriate response except in comparatively
rare cases of grave systemic evil. Though Revelation itself can
probably be largely acquitted of making war on individuals as
opposed to the evil they cause, and is undoubtedly an attack
on what it sees as an evil system, it has to be recognized as a
book that can easily be misused by those who have a psycho-
logical need for enemies – and at some level that may be more
of us than we should like to suppose.

But perhaps the more serious practical problem about
seeing the world in Revelation's conflictual terms is not that
the goodies will be violent towards the baddies, in fact or in
thought, but too *separate* from them. Can we really believe in
such a stark distinction between saints and sinners, and if we
could should we want to?

It is important in addressing this question to be clear about
the distinctions that Revelation is actually making. There is
undoubtedly a great gulf fixed between being inside and
outside, between fighting with the Lamb and fighting against
him, between washing your clothes and staining them; there

could hardly be a more uncompromising statement than in the final chapter:

> Blessed are those who wash their robes, so that they will have the right to the tree of life and may enter the city by the gates. Outside are the dogs and sorcerers and fornicators and murderers and idolaters, and everyone who loves and practises falsehood (22.14–15).

But *who* is inside and who outside? That is very much less clear. There is certainly no assumption that everyone in the Christian community in an 'insider' – indeed it could well be argued that Revelation was only ever written because of John's concern that his communities would lose faith and put themselves 'outside'. The word 'repent' is used far more often in the letters, which are to Christians, than anywhere else in the book. What is more, we need to recognize that for John the horrendous destruction that fills so many chapters, though it is clearly judgment on the world, and entails much suffering for the people in it, is not the final judgment for individuals. We are so prone to think that all our faith must apply to life before death that we need Revelation's reminder that the final judgment comes after it; and we find it portrayed in a scene totally different from the mayhem of the earth's destruction. It is worth quoting at some length:

> Then I saw a great white throne and the one who sat on it; the earth and the heaven fled from his presence, and no place was found for them. And I saw the dead, great and small, standing before the throne, and books were opened. Also another book was opened, the book of life. And the dead were judged according to their works, as recorded in the books. And the sea gave up the dead that were in it, Death and Hades gave up the dead that were in them, and all were judged according to what they had done. Then Death and Hades were thrown into the lake of fire. This is the second death, the lake of fire; and anyone whose name

was not found written in the book of life was thrown into the lake of fire (20.11–15).

A question immediately arises. Why the Lamb's book of life as well as the books with the record of actions? It could be that the former simply summarizes the results of the latter, so that if, as it were, people achieve a pass mark on the examination of what they have done, they get their name put down for heaven. But Revelation, for all its stress on persistent faithfulness, does not see people's ultimate salvation solely in terms of their 'works'. To be in the Lamb's book of life is to be in a life-giving relationship with the Lamb: like the tree of life and the water of life in chapter twenty-two, the book of life *gives* life. This relationship begins in being 'freed from our sins by his blood', and is maintained by faithful following and the continuing washing of one's clothes in the blood of the Lamb (the maintenance, in other words, of one's baptism, with its cleansing and also its commitment).[21] The relationship can be broken by unfaithfulness, which means that one's name is blotted out of the book, but it is always essentially the gift of Christ's love, and who knows where that may be bestowed? (Perhaps even the dogs and sorcerers and fornicators may come into the holy city if they abandon their uncleanness? – the gates, after all, are not shut.)[22] Revelation's parallel judgment books are thus best understood as a refusal to set limits on what Christ's mercy can ultimately do, while still insisting on the consequences of opposition or unfaithfulness to Christ.

But have we resolved the problem merely by allowing that Revelation refuses to pre-empt God's final judgment on people? Is there not also great difficulty in the sharp distinction which Revelation quite clearly does make between *behaviour* which is and is not acceptable? Is this not the way to a narrow-minded sectarianism, which, if it does not wreck churches by its continual carping criticism of brothers and sisters who are not up to scratch, will certainly succeed in making Christians appear to the world as hypocritical bigots who are not to be touched with a barge-pole? Even worse, will it not produce Christians who themselves do not want to touch the world with a barge-pole? When the fall of Babylon is announced, a voice from heaven says:

> Come out of her, my people, so that you do not take part in her sins, and so that you do not share in her plagues; for her sins are heaped high as heaven, and God has remembered her iniquities (18.4–5).

Is this something for the followers of the incarnate and crucified Christ to say? Again, many readers will wonder if this is a part of John that the Lamb has not reached.

Revelation is a passionate book, and its passion is at once its great virtue and its danger. There is great evil in the world which it is all too easy not to see in its true colours, and we need to learn to look at it in Revelation's scarlet and purple, rather than in the shades of grey which lead to endless talk – and no action. It is not wrong to 'come out of' the world if we are going to be corrupted (disarmed, perhaps, in Revelation's metaphor) by staying in; and are we so incorruptible? And how far backward must we bend to get the world to give the gospel a hearing? It is not a sectarian bigot who says, 'Woe to you when all speak well of you . . . blessed are you when people revile you and persecute you and utter all kinds of evil against you falsely'; it is Jesus.[23]

But not all the world is beastly. A view of the world which sees evil everywhere may well be misreading what is only muddle; it will certainly be blind to the grace of God which is at work in the most unlikely places; and perhaps worst of all, it may come positively to rejoice in iniquity. That would be utterly to deny the Lamb, who above all stands for the righteous-making God.

Satan, if we believe Revelation, is a great deceiver, and we may be misled in two different directions. We may go overboard, encouraged perhaps by Revelation, seeing evil everywhere and rejoicing in an angry God who sweeps it all away;

or in the name of moderation we may decide that Revelation's call to arms is much less serious than it really is. But which is the greater danger?

Undoubtedly there are difficulties with Revelation, and readers will decide for themselves how serious they are. But is its alien quality, even its shockingness, altogether problematic? Or is it rather that Revelation is waking us up to a word of God that we might not otherwise hear, and helping us to see what we might otherwise miss? It is in that belief that the last four chapters of this book offer an exploration of how today's Christians might be envisioned by what John has seen.

PART TWO

5

A Vision for the World

In chapter one we said that one of our most urgent needs for the new millennium was a vision with which to begin it. It is now time to ask if Revelation can help us towards such a vision.

A vision for the world needs three elements. First and foremost is the daring imagination of what the world might be – what are we hoping for? (*What* the end of the world is going to be is, after all, considerably more important than *when*.) But vision, if it is to be vision and not mere pipe-dream, needs, secondly, to have some idea of how we might get to where we want to be; and that in turn requires the third element, a realistic appreciation of where we are now. Revelation has all three elements of vision to offer. It has a marvellous picture of the new earth which the world is to become; it has the clearest possible conviction that the end will be reached, together with a picture (though not a map) of the journey and travelling instructions; and it has some powerful if unpalatable pictures of our starting point.

To begin at the end of the book: one of the most striking things about the final chapters of Revelation is that they describe a new *earth*. Revelation has on the whole been given a very wide berth by writers engaging with issues of justice, peace and the integrity of creation, in spite of the fact that they share with the writer of Revelation a deep concern with the future of the world. This is apparently because Revelation is felt to be interested only in the destruction of the earth to make way for an entirely other world. Any such reading does scant justice to the vision of the new Jerusalem with which the book closes. In one sense, it is of course another world: the city comes down from heaven, there is no sun or moon to light it, its dimensions are impossible and its materials almost equally so. But it would be crass to take the description literally, and it would be deeply mistaken to think of the new Jerusalem as totally disconnected from the earth as we know it. For the vision is of *this earth* made new and brought to marvellous fruition. There is the fruitfulness of the natural creation, but wonderfully increased: the tree of life which was in the first garden now brings forth fruit each month (22.2). There is human community, but now brought to its most developed form: the first pair has become a city (21.2). And there is provision for the people of this earth as we know them: the nations are guided by the light of the city (21.24); kings and people have the joy of contributing to it what they have of honour and glory (21.24, 26); there is even healing, from the leaves of the tree of life (22.2). The Old Testament images are everywhere,[1] and with good reason: Revelation inherits the mainstream Jewish conviction that God acts in an earthly setting, not in some realm of disembodied spirits.

To imagine what it would be for a new earth like this to exist presents us with philosophical difficulties akin to those of envisaging a resurrection body for individuals, and a discussion of that is outside the scope of this book. The important point here is that the earth as we know it is *fulfilled* by the new earth, not simply destroyed in its favour. It is not in fact our earth that is to be destroyed, as Revelation sees it, but those who are the destroyers of it:

> . . . your wrath has come, and the time for . . . rewarding your servants . . . and for destroying those who destroy the earth (11.18).

But if the vision of the new earth is to be understood in terms of fulfilment, then it must be of the greatest significance in enlightening us about what our present earth is meant to be and how we are to treat it.

The vision of the city tells us first that human well-being requires community, and not just the satisfaction of individuals' needs. Cities do meet individuals' needs, for it is the mark of a good city to have a multiplicity of opportunities for its citizens to exercise their gifts, pursue their interests, acquire goods and use services. But they are not there simply to allow individual citizens to do their own thing. Cities also provide for people to meet and be together, to act together, and indeed to feel together, or in other words to belong. That is a basic requirement for human beings, not just for their protection where they are weak, but to develop the relatedness that is so large a part of being human. Yet community has to be built; it does not just happen because for reasons of economic necessity people live physically close together. And in today's Western world, community has to be built not only in the face of individual selfishness, but against a prevailing economic system that depends on encouraging people constantly to see themselves in terms of the individual consumer choices they make.

Second, the city is inclusive:

Its gates will never be shut by day, and there will be no night there. People will bring into it the glory and the honour of the nations (21.25–26).

This is partly the inclusiveness of God's generous grace. The gates can surely only be open to let people in (for who would want to go out of such a city?), and there is even a hint in the tree of life with its leaves for the healing of the nations that repentance is an eternal possibility: it appears that the qualification for entry is not fitness but the desire for it. But there is also in the mention of the nations in particular a statement of the city's inclusiveness in terms of race, and indeed of other human groups. This is in fact a keynote of the whole book: the conviction is constantly expressed that God's saving action is for 'every tribe and people and nation and language'. For people who have lived in the century of

Auschwitz and apartheid, and for whom ethnic conflict and racial discrimination still blight every continent, this is a conviction to be taken deeply to heart.

John's inclusiveness needs especial emphasis given the attention that has been attracted by the apparently very *ex*clusive 144,000 in chapter seven, the number of Israelites heard by John to be sealed and saved. This is a prime example of why it is essential to understand the symbolic use of number in Revelation, which we have discussed briefly in chapter three (pp. 35f.). As a literal number, 144,000 is totally irrelevant; rather it is the symbolic number of the perfect community of the people of God, and it is immediately translated into the 'great multitude which no one could number', which is what John sees.[2] This obviously rules out any racial exclusiveness on John's part in favour of the Jews (in which no one who reads his letters to the churches would anyway be likely to believe). But it is surely also a fundamental ruling out of all forms of exclusiveness, even those to which John gives little attention. As we have acknowledged in chapter four, John is, to put it at its most charitable, unaware of gender issues.[3] Nor is he much interested in issues of class: in spite of his very evident suspicion of the powerful, he shows no sign of thinking that the categories of 'small' and 'great', who figure equally among the saints and those subject to the destruction of God, should be abolished.[4] But John's relative blindness to what are issues for us need not stop us learning from him the basic value of inclusiveness. Nor should it: inclusiveness is something our world needs desperately to learn.

But inclusiveness is not the only value suggested by the vision of people bringing into the city 'the glory and the honour of the nations'. In a book which presents God as utterly glorious, and insists time after time that he alone is to be worshipped, nevertheless real glory and honour are to be found in human beings, and in the natural creation. When they enter the new Jerusalem, people do not toss away as worthless what they thought was honourable and glorious; they bring it in, for it has a place there. It is easy to think that

Revelation has a low view of the creation, and of humanity within it, when so much of it is so apparently easily consigned to destruction, but the very reverse is the case. Essentially, as we have seen, earth is to be saved from those who would destroy it; and there can scarcely be a higher view of human beings than to suppose them capable of reigning with Christ.[5] Certainly they must be redeemed before this can be so, but a reading of Revelation which treats the saints as if they were a totally different order of being from everybody else is quite untrue to the book's fundamental vision in chapters four and five, which is of creation and redemption held together in the heart of God. Redemption restores and fulfils creation, but it can in no way deny or undervalue it. In the very first picture of the worship of heaven in chapter four the worshippers sing:

> You are worthy, our Lord and God, to receive glory and honour and power, for you created all things, and by your will they existed and were created (4.11).

So the third thing to say about the city is that it is a place where the fundamental value of the natural creation and of human beings is recognized, and its potential brought to fulfilment. And to live by this vision on this earth will mean cherishing and nurturing all that realizes that potential.

It would be a mistake, however, to understand the ideal of human flourishing in purely humanistic terms. It is easy for Western Christians to suppose that fullness of life is really about ensuring that everyone has a right and proper share of God's created gifts. Undoubtedly that is part of the truth; but it is not the whole of it. When the kings and people bring into the city the honour and glory of the nations, they are bringing it into a city filled with the light and the presence of God; it is impossible not to hear overtones of offering and of worship, of the three kings bringing their costly gifts at the beginning of the earthly story of the Lamb. Fullness of life requires not just an enjoyment of the good things of creation, but an understanding of them as gift, and a relationship of loving worship with the giver. The poor, paradoxically perhaps, are often much more aware of this relationship, and in this respect have a fuller life than the rich, who may need to catch from this vision a realization of what they lack as well as of what they unfairly enjoy. The city is not only a city of inclusive community and the flourishing of the creation; it is a city of worship. That is the final thing to say about the city – or in one sense the first, for the relationship with the God who dwells in the city is the key to the whole of its life.

But what is Revelation's vision of the way to the heavenly city? To get a clear picture of this it may be best to look first at the third element in vision which we identified, the realistic appreciation of the situation in which the world currently is. Here we have to dare to be truthful. There is a great deal about truthfulness in Revelation, and it is probably not an exaggeration to say that in John's view, to lie is the most serious of all sins. At the end of the colourful description of those who cannot enter the heavenly city – 'the dogs and sorcerers and fornicators and murderers and idolaters' – come the words 'and everyone who loves and practises falsehood' (22.15). Many readers of Revelation have recoiled from its emphasis on the sinfulness and potential for disaster in the world; but is John wrong in thinking that human beings often need to be *forced* to see the truth? We can be wonderfully blind to truths which we do not wish to see.

One of those truths is that sin has consequences. As we discussed in chapter four (pp. 51ff.), the wrath of God, or of the Lamb, is an idea with which many Christians today have acute difficulty; but in so far as it says that God allows us to be brought up against the results of our own sinfulness, it holds a truth that the problems of today's world suggest we badly need. If we refuse to take responsibility for the predicament we are in, we shall never make the changes upon which the world's well-being, and perhaps survival, depends. In theological terms, one of the ways in which we may be brought to repentance is by encountering the wrath of God – or by being warned of it. And if it is objected that the sequences of seven seals, trumpets and bowls sound much more like the prediction of what is inevitable than the warning of what may be avoided, we should remember John's interest in, and belief in, repentance. The wrath of God is inexorable, but it is not inescapable for those who will repent. John, it must be said, does not expect repentance, but it is possible – and sometimes comes.[6] To see the truth of where we are, in other words, may genuinely be the start of the journey to the end we hope to reach.

But Revelation has more to show us than the fact that sin has consequences, which for some readers may remain a rather abstract idea (though powerfully resonating for others with their own experience). We are shown also how easily we are caught up in the world's sin. No one can read the descriptions of the beast in chapter thirteen or the destruction of the harlot Babylon in chapter eighteen without feeling how forcefully seductive power and wealth can be:

> In amazement the whole earth followed the beast. They worshipped the dragon, for he had given his authority to the beast, and they worshipped the beast, saying, 'Who is like the beast, and who can fight against it?' (13.3b–4).

> And the merchants of the earth weep and mourn for her, since no one buys their cargo any more, cargo of gold, silver, jewels and pearls, fine linen, purple, silk and scarlet, all kinds of scented wood, all articles of ivory, all articles of costly wood, bronze, iron, and marble, cinnamon, spice, incense, myrrh, frankincense, wine, olive oil, choice flour and wheat, cattle and sheep, horses and chariots, slaves – and human lives. 'The fruit for which your soul longed has gone from you, and all your dainties and your splendour are lost to you, never to be found again!' (18.11–14).

The root of John's ferocity is not a rejection of all human authority, or a puritanical suspicion of the world's good things; if that were the case, the kings of the earth would not bring their glory into the heavenly city. He is angry at the giving of ultimate value to what is not ultimate, at that untruthfulness which is idolatry: power and wealth belong first to God. And he wants above all to expose that untruthfulness: the worship of the beast is only sustained by the *deception* of the second beast which is allowed to perform great signs, and so persuade the inhabitants of the earth to make an image of the beast, and even to make the image come alive.[7] People can be made to believe all this, but *it is not true*: only God deserves worship. Similarly the overweening confidence of the harlot in her own power has no basis in reality:

> Since in her heart she says, 'I rule as a queen; I am no widow, and I will never see grief', therefore her plagues will come in a single day – pestilence and mourning and famine – and she will be burned with fire, for mighty is the Lord God who judges her (18.7b–8).

Just as seeing that sin has consequences may lead to a change of heart in the world in general, so becoming conscious of our own implication in the idolatries of earth is meant to lead to a change of heart in us. No one can read the letters to the churches, with their repeated calls to repent, and suppose that the call to 'come out of her, my people, so that you do not take part in her sins' (18.4) is not most seriously meant. As we have seen in chapter four (pp. 62ff.), the call to remove oneself from the world is problematic for us, and we shall need to discuss it further in chapter eight. Here it is sufficient to note the strength of the attraction of the world's power and wealth to Christians, and the ease with which we are deceived in these matters. We are so accustomed to thinking of a gap between the church and the world which we are not good at crossing with our values and our message, that it may have escaped us that the world is often very effective indeed at getting its message and its values into the church.

Most readers of Revelation will find its first kind of

envisioning far more palatable than its second. To be grasped by a vision of the heavenly city offers us a way out of cynicism and hopelessness; and we would gladly take it. To contemplate the evil in the world, especially as something that infects ourselves, is highly uncomfortable. Part of our discomfort is doubtless the pride that does not wish to admit our need for repentance. But perhaps there is also a fearful doubt that anything can be done about the world's evil. People will never be motivated, we fear, by anything other than their desire for power and wealth: what chance is there of their learning from the consequences of their sin? What chance is there, when you come down to it, of *our* turning our backs on it? The heavenly city is unattainable, the journey there a virtual non-starter. If we are to be convinced otherwise, we need the final element in the vision, of the way from what is to what will be.

A vision of the world's moving from its present state to the bliss of the heavenly city is shown to us at two levels in Revelation. At the cosmic level, it happens in the defeat of evil by God through the Lamb. With all the doubts that some people have felt about seeing the world in terms of a simple conflict between good and evil, it is obvious that if the life of the heavenly city is to become a reality, all that is contrary to or less than that life has somehow to cease to be. For John, who embraces the language of conquering without a qualm, this means the victory of the Lamb. At the end of the sequences of seals and trumpets we are shown those who oppose him cowering in terror,[8] while heaven celebrates because:

> the kingdom of the world has become the kingdom of our Lord and of his Messiah, and he will reign forever and ever (11.15).

Similar worship choruses celebrating the Lamb punctuate the warfare as it reaches its climax. Following the destruction of Babylon, we see the kings of the earth gathered to make war against the Word of God, and utterly defeated by him; then the beasts and the dragon, the powers behind the world's evil, are consigned to the lake of fire.

At the more personal level, the way from the world as it is to the world as it will be is following the Lamb and sharing his victory. For the Christian, as for Christ, warfare and conquering are the categories in which John works. It is this language above all which unites the letters to the churches with the visions that follow – and indeed with the vision that precedes the letters, for the Christ who is seen among the lampstands in chapter one as Lord of the church has a sharp, two-edged sword coming from his mouth (1.16). Each letter ends with a promise made 'to everyone who conquers', and *the* question therefore for John's readers is whether or not they are among the conquerors. To be so is clearly not to avoid suffering, or even apparent defeat: in chapter six those who have been martyred are told to wait until their number is made complete by the martyrdom of others; in chapter twelve the dragon makes war on the children of the woman representing the church; while in chapters eleven and thirteen the 'witnesses' and then the saints are conquered and killed by the beast.[9] But, even more clearly, ultimately Revelation sees the saints as conquerors, provided that they remain faithful to the Lamb whom they follow.

This third element in Revelation's vision is perhaps the most difficult to take on board. Unlike the vision of the heavenly city, it is not wholly attractive, for, deeply reassuring though the idea of the sweeping away of evil may be, the language in which it is described jars upon many readers for reasons which were explored in chapter four. Unlike the vision of the present predicament in which the world finds itself, it is not immediately comprehensible, and so cannot be convincing. What does the victory of the Lamb mean, and is it believable?

There are two key passages in Revelation for understanding the victory of the Lamb, both accounts of visions. One holds what might be called the historical key, though the vision is couched not in terms of historical event, but in the inner 'heavenly' meaning of it. The historical key is the death of Christ on the cross, which is described in chapter twelve as a war between Michael and his angels on the one hand and the dragon and his angels on the other. The dragon is defeated and thrown down from heaven to earth, where what might be called his death-throes are violent but short-lived. The war is in fact more a court-room battle than a military engagement: Satan is defeated as 'accuser of our comrades (Gk "brothers")' so that the reference is to the death of Christ as gaining us the forgiveness of our sins (with Michael acting as it were as counsel for the defence). In terms of the ultimate reality which heaven represents,[10] Satan has no more that he can do: evil will always be unable to withstand Christ when it encounters him. Nevertheless evil on earth is still real. It is an insight of Revelation, as of Paul's theology, that evil done has evil consequences, and they have to be lived through, by those who have 'conquered him (i.e. Satan) by the blood of the Lamb' (12.11) as well as by those who have not.[11]

Victory in this sense may seem to be victory with a very big 'if'. What if evil does not encounter Christ? – will it not continue to reign as unchallenged as many people looking at today's world might suppose it does? This is where the other key passage comes in, which offers what might be called the theological key: the vision in chapter five of the slaughtered Lamb taking the scroll from God's hand.

The vision is wonderfully paradoxical: the Lamb is *standing* as though it had been *slaughtered*. Slaughtered lambs do not stand; they collapse helpless in a bloody heap. Equally, standing lambs have suffered no slaughter; in apocalyptic imagery, as we have seen, they are quite fearsome beasts, with no trace of the cuddly bundle in the shepherd's arms. In the Lamb who both stands and is slaughtered is the essence of the mystery of the victory of the cross. If slaughter cannot fell the lamb, it will stand for ever and be utterly invincible; evil may attack it with all that it has, but it will in the end exhaust itself and the Lamb will still be standing. But if the standing Lamb bears the marks of slaughter, then the Lamb's victory will be won not by any violence, but by its complete opposite – the acceptance of violence done to the Lamb, to the ultimate point of death.

But how do we know that this is real victory, the real defeat of evil, and not just eternal suffering on the Lamb's part? We have here to draw on two ideas, one of which is taken for granted in Revelation and one of which it is concerned to express with all the emphasis at its command. The first is what may be called the linear idea of time – that history is going somewhere, rather than just going round in circles. The end of time is shrouded in mystery in the Bible, but nowhere is there any doubt that there will be an end – the Day of the Lord in the Old Testament, or the Kingdom of God in the New will surely come. The end may, as we have seen, be in some sense a fulfilment of the beginning – paradise not simply restored, but taken into a new dimension – but it is distinct from it, and there is no going back. Revelation is very deeply rooted in its own scriptural tradition, and it is imbued from start to finish with this 'sense of an ending'.[12] The second idea, equally traditional but more overtly emphasized in Revelation, is the theological idea that God is sovereign. God alone is to be worshipped, and in the end nothing and no one can withstand his will. The difficulties that many people today find with such an idea have been discussed in chapter four (pp. 53ff.); here we have simply to affirm that *some* understanding of the sovereignty of God has to be accepted if Revelation's vision is to mean anything at all. But if God's will in the end must be done, and there is in fact going to be an end, then victory for God is certain, and it is equally certain for anyone who is working with and for him. The other feature, therefore, to notice about the vision of the Lamb in chapter five is that the Lamb 'went and took the scroll from the right hand of the one who was seated on the throne' (5.7). This parallels other biblical passages where people are presented to God, or are in some other way authorized by him before acting on his behalf, and there is always the idea not only that they are being authorized, but empowered: they cannot fail. Nor can the Lamb, and that means not only that evil cannot defeat him, it cannot hide from him either: it must itself be defeated.[13]

How the Lamb's victory is won remains surprisingly unclear. Very little of the destruction of the book is directly attributable to him,[14] and there are in fact relatively few points at which he is directly active at all; the focus is often, rather, on his receiving worship and praise in heaven. Where he does act, it is in ways that have a clear link to the incarnate Christ, or in what might be called human ways. It is his sacrificial death which sets in motion the whole grand movement towards the End. Where he appears, not under the name of the Lamb, but as one like the Son of Man in the midst of the lampstands in chapter one, or as the Word of God in chapter nineteen, his weapon is the sharp sword which comes out of his mouth. The Lamb, in other words, speaks the truth and he suffers to the point of death. This is his part in the victory of God, and John is content to leave within the mystery of God how it is that it becomes victory. We are being offered vision, not proof.

If the Lamb's followers are content to accept this vision, then it becomes immensely powerful for them personally. If it is truthfulness and the willingness to pay its price that wins victory, then that is a victory that can be shared by the Lamb's brothers and sisters. And in fact it is a key part of Revelation's vision that the Lamb and the saints do appear together in victory. The saints are the Lamb's army, who have washed their robes in the blood of the Lamb and now stand with him on Mount Zion, they sing the song of Moses and of the Lamb in heaven, and they follow the Word of God to make final war on the beast and the kings of the earth.[15] Readers of the letters to the churches may be struck by an apparent contrast between the warlike 'conquering' language and what the churches are actually being told to do – which is on the whole to resist error, and to endure. But what is required of them is what has been required of Christ before them. Truthful speech and endurance may not be dramatic, or seem effective, but they are what God uses in his victory. John wants his people to see that.

Quite clearly, however, the saints are not being presented with an easy option, and there remains the question for many readers of whether they can see themselves in this role. If they cannot, then Revelation becomes a frightening book, for the only alternative to being a saint is to find a place among God's enemies. If that is where they see themselves, most people will simply shut the book and hope it is not true. Here we need to cling to the opening chapter of Revelation, with its description of Christ as the one 'who loves us and freed us from our sins by his blood, and made us to be a kingdom, priests serving his God and Father' (1.5b–6). The Lamb still stands for those who want to be his followers, as well as for the world; neither for the world nor for themselves should the readers of Revelation give up hope.

What would the consequences be for the church today of seeing the world with Revelation's eyes? The whole of the rest of this book addresses that question, but it may be helpful here to make some summary introductory points. Some are expanded in the next three chapters, but many will be left for readers to develop themselves.

Perhaps the first thing to say is that to have a vision at all of what the world could be is something to be cherished. We live in an age which invests considerable time, money and energy in the art of persuading people, and we are well aware that nothing persuades so much as conviction; at the same time conviction is hard to come by when values are felt to be merely individual preferences, all right no doubt for those who subscribe to them, but in no sense of universal application. In an age which, perhaps regretfully, feels that it has outgrown ideals, the church is called to be unashamedly idealistic. The world needs the conviction of those who believe that their idealism is realism, because it takes God seriously into account, both his values and his power.

Secondly, Christians have to abandon more completely the heresy that religion has nothing to do with politics. The vision of the new Jerusalem says that God has a will for the earth;

and the affairs of the polis (city) are dealt with by politics. We discuss in greater detail in chapter eight what this might mean for church life, and the demands it will make upon us, not least the need to act ourselves on what we tell others they should be doing. Meanwhile, we may summarize here the basic values which Revelation would lead us to take into political judgment and action. One will be a care for the environment, not over against human beings on the one hand, nor simply as the home of human beings on the other (important though that is, especially for future generations), but as the intrinsically valuable gift of a creator God. Another value, needing special emphasis in our individualist age, is the value for community, at a variety of levels, local, national and global. There will be also the value for inclusiveness, which will raise for British Christians issues of social exclusion in general, and racism in particular. Finally there will be the value for human well-being, with all the issues that will raise about what truly makes for human well-being, who is to judge, and how far judgments may properly be imposed on those who do not share them. The urgent task of addressing the injustices of the world economic system arises here (as it does also on the grounds of inclusiveness). But so does the task of gaining recognition for people's non-material needs.

In pursuing many of these values Christians will find allies, among people of other faiths, or of no faith. But it takes very little thought to realize that we shall be led to conclusions that are unpopular with others and may be uncongenial to ourselves. A real value for community, for example, would surely require a substantial shift in most people's attitudes to paying rates and taxes? To tackle racism within the white community will require a willingness to be challenged and to change that most people will find extremely hard. Valuing other people's well-being and the environment may ask quite substantial changes in life-style and the sacrifice of comfort and convenience. So a third characteristic of a church envisioned by Revelation will be willingness to learn to see and tell unpalatable truths, and to live with the consequences. A church which sees the world truthfully and discerns what must be done in the light of God's ultimate purpose for the world will not be an easy church to live with, either for those outside it or for those who belong to it.

If that church, however, has caught the vision of the Lamb triumphant, it will have the final characteristic of confidence. The confidence will not be in terms of what the church knows it can achieve by truth-telling and enduring love, for that is God's business. Nor will it be the confidence of being able to predict what God will do to make the Lamb's victory real, for Revelation does not tell us that, in other than highly symbolic picture language. Rather, the church's confidence will be grounded in its vision of who God is: the sovereign God of the Lamb. It is that God who determines what ultimately happens to the world, just as it is the vision of what God is which underpins all envisioning of the world, in its present and its future. And it is to that fundamental vision that we turn in the next chapter.

6

Worship: Learning to See

If we were allowed only one key to the understanding of Revelation, we should have to choose 'worship'. The worship keynote is sounded right at the beginning of John's account of what he has seen: 'I was in the Spirit on the Lord's day' (by implication, among the Lord's people at worship) (1.10). Not only does John see as he worships, worship is what he sees, and hears, at all the key points in the book. The foundation visions of God and of the Lamb in chapters four and five are essentially visions of the worship of heaven, culminating in the worship song:

> To the one seated on the throne and to the Lamb be blessing and honour and glory and might for ever and ever! (5.13).

And glimpses of heavenly worship, with similar worship choruses, as we might call them, follow at regular intervals throughout the book.

Often these choruses are comments on what has been happening, either in heaven or on earth, and as such they function rather like the choruses in classical Greek plays, which are a device used to tell the audience what has been going on off-stage and what it is appropriate to feel about it. But Revelation's choruses are *worship* choruses, because that expresses John's conviction that it is as people worship that they see, and so can tell, the truth. What is more, much of the truth that is seen concerns worship. Worship is a large part of the message of Revelation, in other words, as well as of its content and its context. On the one hand is the sovereign God who alone and above all is to be worshipped. On the other are human beings, for whom worship is the fundamental purpose of their existence.[1] Worship is at the heart of life in the eternal city:

> . . . the throne of God and of the Lamb will be in it, and his servants will worship him; they will see his face, and his name will be on their foreheads (22.3b–4).

And worship of the sovereign God is central to life on earth too. False worship is deadly, as we shall see later in this chapter. But it is easy. Even John is tempted to pay undue reverence to the angels who show or interpret his visions to him, and in a signal of the book's fundamental message is told, 'You must not do that! . . . Worship God.'[2]

Christians have always realized that worship both reflects and in turn forms belief. A study of the worship choruses in Revelation is therefore a good way into understanding what John himself believes and wants his people to believe too. The very first one expresses two great complementary beliefs about God which inform the whole book:

> Day and night without ceasing they sing, 'Holy, holy, holy, the Lord God, the Almighty, who was and is and is to come' (4.8).

God is in a wholly different world of purity and power from ours, and yet he is *'to come'*. Had the sentence finished 'and is to be', as we might have expected, we should not yet know whether this high and holy God was concerned with us; but if he is to come, then from the beginning we do know that he wishes to have dealings with us – and that therefore we have to do with him. The fundamental nature of the relationship is established in the chorus which follows almost immediately:

> You are worthy, our Lord and God, to receive glory and
> honour and power, for you created all things, and by your
> will they existed and were created (4.11).

There is here the total dependence of the created world upon
God, yet at the same time also the basis for God's interest
in his world; to quote an insight from a different part of
scripture, he can hate nothing that he has made.[3] But something much more positive than that emerges very quickly from
the worship in Revelation: the Lamb appears, sharing wholly
in the glory of God, and yet to be worshipped precisely
because of what he has done for created beings:

> You are worthy to take the scroll and to open its seals, for
> you were slaughtered and by your blood you ransomed for
> God saints from every tribe and language and people and
> nation; you have made them to be a kingdom and priests
> serving our God, and they will reign on earth (5.9).

What is given priority even over the effect of the Lamb's
action is the manner of it, utterly paradoxical for one who
shares God's glory: 'you were slaughtered'. But the paradoxical truth is immediately repeated, as heaven, joined here
uniquely by earth, unites the Lamb with God himself in equal
praise:

> Worthy is the Lamb that was slaughtered to receive power
> and wealth and wisdom and might and honour and glory
> and blessing! . . . To the one seated on the throne and to the
> Lamb be blessing and honour and glory and might for ever
> and ever! (5.12–13).

What Christ has done for the saints is again ascribed both to
God and to the Lamb in the heavenly worship of the 'great
multitude that no one could count':

> Salvation belongs to our God who is seated on the throne,
> and to the Lamb! (7.10).

But this salvation is not just for individuals; it is for the whole earth. Towards the end of the series of trumpet judgments the heavenly chorus says:

> The kingdom of the world has become the kingdom of our Lord and of his Messiah, and he will reign forever and ever (11.15).

But this salvation cannot be good news for those who do not want it. What is created is created by God's will, and, in Revelation's theology, it follows that he will not allow his good purpose for it finally to be thwarted. Hence the judgment on, and in the end the destruction of, what denies the life that God has given. Straight after the joyful greeting for the 'kingdom of our Lord and of his Messiah', the elders in heaven sing:

> We give you thanks, Lord God Almighty, who are and who were, for you have taken your great power and begun to reign. The nations raged, but your wrath has come, and the time for judging the dead, for rewarding your servants, the prophets and saints and all who fear your name, both small and great, and for destroying those who destroy the earth (11.17–18).

This is the rejoicing of those who have hungered and thirsted to see right prevail, and have endured much suffering while the unrighteous have apparently triumphed.[4] Christians today who have been insulated from the world's wrongs perhaps are over-sensitive to the note of vengeance in the words, and underestimate the longing for the end of what destroys the earth. For those who destroy are the enemies of God, and not just of the saints; and in a fallen world there can be no justice without judgment. Even where the worship more frankly exults in the punishment of the wicked –

> he has judged the great whore who corrupted the earth with her fornication, and he has avenged on her the blood of his servants (19.2) –

the 'bottom line' is rejoicing in the triumph of good:

> Hallelujah! For the Lord our God the Almighty reigns (19.6).[5]

In Revelation's worship, to summarize, we are confronted with God's transcendent power and glory, which, brought to bear upon the world that he has made, we may call his sovereignty: God is always on his throne. It is the will of this sovereign God to make the world a place where goodness reigns; and his means of doing so is by the self-sacrifice of Christ, the slaughtered Lamb. Through Christ, people may return to God and become a part of his action in the world, as his servants and even as rulers. But if they do not do so they will encounter the judgment of God – they will not ultimately be allowed to defeat God's intention. Yet what defeats them remains the goodness of the sovereign Lord and the slaughtered Lamb, before whom all heaven bows in adoration.

As we have said, it is the function of the worship scenes within the book to sum up the action at important points, and it is therefore no surprise at all to find that what the worship in Revelation says about God, the church and the world is just what the book as a whole says about these things. But it is very significant that John chooses to highlight his message in this particular way. If the book is a revelation, an envisioning, and that vision is supremely of worship, does that not suggest that, of all human activities, worship is what should most have the quality of envisioning us? Is not worship where 'heaven breaks through' – or even, to put it in temporal terms, where 'the end is near'? It may well be, in fact, that Revelation itself was first read, and heard, in a worship setting. Certainly it has many echoes of what we know of early Christian worship, not least of eucharistic worship, where there has always been an emphasis on looking forward to Christ's return.[6] But wherever it is read, the whole book breathes the conviction that to worship is to put oneself in the way of seeing.

It is important, however, to understand what this seeing

means for John. It is easy to think of visions as extraordinary mystical experiences which do not necessarily connect very much with everyday living. Whatever extraordinary experiences John may have had, he was entirely clear that they constituted a *prophetic* vision, which others must share not so much that they might wonder at it (though wonder has to be appropriate), but so that they could live by it.[7] Some of the final words of the book give a sense of his urgency about this:

> See, I am coming soon! Blessed is the one who keeps the words of the prophecy of this book (22.7).

As with vision, so with worship. For some people at some times worship is a mystical experience. More regularly it is where people see the truth of what is, and by expressing that truth come to believe it more securely. But it would be a dangerous half-truth to stop there. Revelation is full of the conviction which John's Gospel expresses by saying that the truth is to be *done*; seeing which does not lead to doing is bogus, or at least essentially incomplete. Worship must relate to doing.

This emphasis on doing as well as seeing sheds light on the way in which the saints appear in Revelation's pictures of heavenly worship, either as themselves the worshippers, or as those who are rejoiced over when they are vindicated or rewarded. An example is the verse already quoted which rejoices that 'prophets and saints and all who fear your name, both small and great' are finally being rewarded for what they have done (11.18); another is the passage where God prepares for the final judgment of the bowls, the seven last plagues, and those who have 'conquered the beast' sing:

> Great and amazing are your deeds, Lord God the Almighty! Just and true are your ways, King of the nations! . . . (15.3).

It is easy for today's readers, especially those from cultures where to claim merit for oneself is not done, to see this as a rather smug rejoicing on the part of goodies who have come out on top; but it is surely intended as an encouragement of faithful servants who may feel themselves to be working very hard and achieving nothing. John's vision validates their service in the strongest possible way, by bringing it into the worship of heaven. There is a place in worship, in other words, for the offering of God's servants. So 'learning to see' in worship, in the words of the title of this chapter, will be learning to see not only what is (about God and the world, and yourself), but also what you must do and how you may do it.

Before considering what all this might mean for Christian worship today, we need to look at another element in Revelation's understanding of worship. Heaven being the place both of worship and of truth, its worship is, obviously, true worship; but earth may be, and often is, the place of worship that is essentially false.[8] As with true worship, not only rites are involved, with the thoughts and feelings that go with them; worship is also what people do. In chapter thirteen there is a fearsome picture of false worship, which is worth quoting at some length:

> And I saw a beast rising out of the sea; and on its horns were ten diadems, and on its heads were blasphemous names . . . And the dragon gave it his power and his throne and great authority. One of its heads seemed to have received a death-blow, but its mortal wound had been healed. In amazement the whole earth followed the beast. They worshipped the dragon, for he had given his authority to the beast, and they worshipped the beast, saying 'Who is like the beast, and who can fight against it?' The beast was given a mouth uttering haughty and blasphemous words, and it was allowed to exercise authority for forty-two months. It opened its mouth to utter blasphemies against God, blaspheming his name and his dwelling, that is, those who dwell in heaven. Also it was allowed to make war on the saints and to conquer them. It was given authority over every tribe and people and language and nation, and all the

inhabitants of the earth will worship it, everyone whose name has not been written from the foundation of the world in the book of life of the Lamb that was slaughtered . . . Then I saw another beast that rose out of the earth; it had two horns like a lamb and it spoke like a dragon. It exercises all the authority of the first beast on its behalf, and it makes the earth and its inhabitants worship the first beast, whose mortal wound had been healed. It performs great signs, even making fire come down from heaven to earth in the sight of all; and by the signs that it is allowed to perform on behalf of the beast, it deceives the inhabitants of earth, telling them to make an image for the beast that had been wounded by the sword and yet lived; and it was allowed to give breath to the image of the beast so that the image of the beast could even speak and cause those who would not worship the image of the beast to be killed. Also it causes all, both small and great, both rich and poor, both free and slave, to be marked on the right hand or the forehead, so that no one can buy or sell who does not have the mark, that is the name of the beast or the number of its name (13.1–17).

What is all this about? Commentators vary as to how much they think it is directly about the Roman empire, and how much it is a more spiritual description of the Antichrist who may be seen in any earthly power setting itself up against God.[9] Certainly there are details very suggestive of Rome – the seven heads being seven Roman emperors, the wound of which the beast is healed being the emperor Nero's suicide and the expectation that he would reappear, and so on. But careful examination of these details shows that they do not fit at all perfectly,[10] and in any case, isn't John being more profound than simply giving a coded description of one set of political circumstances? We have at work in this passage what commentators have called the 'Satanic trinity' – the devil (dragon) and his beasts parodying, indeed masquerading as, God, Christ and the Spirit; that must be about more than just Rome.[11]

Perhaps our interpretative key of spiritual insides and material outsides can help us here. John urgently wants people to see the spiritual significance of the political situation in which they are living, and that means painting a word-picture for them which at one and the same time will remind them of outward circumstances on the one hand and illuminate for them on the other what is going on spiritually. Today's readers may note for interest the indications of the Roman situation that the passage gives; but what will be really in the spirit of John's writing will be to look for what in today's world is falsely claiming our worship, and how. What might the passage have to say about that?

What is immediately noticeable is the very close connection between what is worshipped and what is powerful. 'They worshipped the beast, saying "Who is like the beast, and who can fight against it?".' Power is not only feared, it attracts: as John puts it, 'in amazement the whole earth followed the beast'; we might more prosaically observe that the powerful always have hangers-on. Translate fear into awe and attraction into desire for what is beyond us, and we are talking about worship. Of course believers in the Christian God kneel, literally or metaphorically, to one who is all-holy as well as all-powerful, and we should want to maintain firmly that might must be right before it is to be worshipped – but we have to recognize that people have always knelt to kings as well as to God, and that it is perilously easy to kneel to might alone. So there is always a question to be asked about what we see as having power over us – because it is very likely that we are worshipping it. We shall explore this a little later on.

Secondly, there is often, if not always, an element of force alongside the attractiveness of power and where the power is resisted the force element comes into its own – hence the beast making war on the saints and conquering them, whereas the non-resistant experience it rather as authority (13.7). But what is even more striking is that the worship of power is maintained by lies and deception. This is a large part of the work of the second, earth beast, which parodies the work of the Holy Spirit. Whereas the Holy Spirit leads people into all the truth,[12] the second beast gets the worship of the dragon and the first beast into people's hearts and minds by performing false 'miracles' (13.13–15). In John's time this is directed at the propagandists of the emperor cult; we might think of political propaganda, or advertising.[13]

Thirdly, it is interesting to notice the economic 'postscript' to the passage: no one can buy or sell without having the beast's mark (13.17). It is easy to read this passage as being about political power, and to see chapter eighteen as a separate treatment of economic domination, in the lament (or taunt song) over the fall of the harlot city Babylon. But there is in fact the realization here how 'powerful' economics are; the earth beast has to control the economy as well as propaganda if it is to keep the worship of the sea beast and the dragon in good order.

Before leaving this passage, there is one final point to make, which is made clear by the inclusion of the economic postscript. If you cannot go to the shops unless you are a bona fide worshipper, then worship clearly in one way or another covers the whole of everyday life. Which means, to put it the other way round, that the whole of life has the deepest spiritual significance. Whatever puts people in the power of the beasts is in the end blasphemy and devil worship: to worship the beast *is* to worship the dragon (13.4). For the truth is that God is sovereign, and that his sovereignty extends to the whole of what he has created; to attribute power to any other place is a lie, and is false worship, of the devil. It is John's genius that alongside his sublime pictures of heavenly worship he has the keenest possible sense that the whole of earthly life is worship too – for good or ill.

If we are to follow Revelation in seeing the whole of life in terms of worship, it may be helpful to start with this very wide-angled lens, and ask whether our society encourages, or even forces, us into false worship in everyday life. We have here to return to the discussion of chapter one, which identified a widespread sense of powerlessness as being characteristic of today's world. Is this powerlessness something we uniformly regret or resent, or are there things which we see as powerful which we are prone to worship?

A complete answer to that question would include some purely personal responses, and some that depended on being a member of a particular group, as well as some of much more universal application. A book like this can use only a very broad brush, and go for what must surely be the primary candidate for false worship for Western Christians: money. (The word is used in the broad sense of that system of values and practices of which money in the narrow sense, currency, is at the heart.) People have always, of course, found money attractive, but *now it is a world power*. Through the money markets, and the transnational companies and commercial banks over which national governments have such imperfect control, we have created a system which has real power over us.

By and large we collude with this. Those who will not follow the dictates of the money markets go out of business, and can no longer buy or sell. So most people follow money in amazement all over the world, and say 'Who can fight against it?' It may force us into business practices which we regret (we can see that competition, for example, may have very unfortunate results) – but we see no alternative. Thus employment goes to where there is the best return on capital, not where there is the greatest need for work; and international debt makes war, if not on the saints, certainly on the poor, who, having no weapons to use against it, are conquered and suffer the consequences in life-denying poverty. All this is kept going by vast amounts of money and energy invested in propaganda designed to persuade us of the desirability of money and what it can buy. Economic growth becomes something of unquestioned value, and it is almost never asked whether its costs are too high, far less whether its benefits are real. Few people ask whether consumers genuinely want what they can be persuaded to buy, far less whether it is for their well-being. There is a wilful blindness about this that arouses the suspicion that the inhabitants of the earth are being deceived, and deceived into false worship. Several commentators have noted the religious overtones in much of our pursuit of material good (with shopping malls as our cathedrals, for example); and this 'religion' is idolatry.[14]

But it is important to see that Revelation offers more than just a good line in pulpit denunciation aimed at inducing guilt. Certainly the book looks for a response from its readers, and very probably a changing of their ways, but if we take seriously the analysis of the 'powers' described in chapter three, then it also offers a diagnosis of our predicament so that we can understand what we are up against. In an important book which analyses today's global capitalism and looks for Christian alternatives, Ulrich Duchrow gives a bleak picture of the effects of globalization of capital, but at the same time emphasizes that we are not simply talking about individuals' sins:

> It can be demonstrated that the . . . mechanisms [of market de-regulation] are causing the pauperization of the majority of human beings and the destruction of the environment, and at the same time bringing increased wealth to a minority. It is not greedy individuals causing the change, but a new mode of capital accumulation and de-regulation.[15]

But if our situation is one of 'structural evil', what response to it is required from individuals? Even if the saints learn from Revelation to see the world as caught up in idolatry by its economic system, what are they supposed to do then? Are they not in fact hopelessly compromised if, as most Western Christians do, they benefit from that system?

False guilt is deeply paralyzing, so it may help first of all to repeat that there is an element of powerlessness in the position of affluent Christians; it is not only the poor who are powerless, though they suffer vastly more for their powerlessness. We waste energy in feeling guilty about living under a system which we cannot in any serious degree change; even national governments cannot do so, according to Duchrow, who is specifically looking for alternatives to the present world economic system:

> ... it must ... be said that the *option of a wholesale transformation of society* is out of the question ... At present there is no slot available for a nation to set up a genuine alternative, untouched by the global market or even partially autonomous.[16]

To say that we cannot do everything, however, is by no means to say that we can do nothing. The idolatry of the system in which we live is not *totally* irresistible, and if we are not doing what we can to resist it, we fall into worship of what has power over us. Then there is a proper guilt, of which we cannot absolve ourselves. We have to recognize how easy such worship is, and how hard the resistance, when it is so likely to be deeply contrary to our natural inclinations and material interests.[17] Even establishing a serious wish to challenge the system will be difficult, before we tackle any of the practical questions as to what is to be done. Certainly this is not something which can properly be left to individual consciences. Not only are the issues of structural evil too large for the church as a whole to duck the responsibility of responding to them; it is part of learning to be realistic about the more-than-individual nature of the world's predicament to begin to take seriously ways of corporate response.

There is a large and challenging agenda for the church here, of which we shall say more in the final chapter. From the point of view of worship, the real significance of this consideration of our world's economic system has been to illustrate Revelation's conviction that the whole of life is to be understood in terms of worship. It is now time to ask what effect this insight, and the rest of what Revelation has to show us about worship, might have on what goes on in church on Sundays.

If we understand the whole of life as worship, with God

present in it all as the one to whom life is offered, then worship services will not be an addition to daily living so much as an intensification of it: both our daily lives and the God to whom we offer them are as it were highlighted by what we do in worship. This has two sides to it – the bringing into worship of every part of our daily life, and the preparation of ourselves to receive whatever experience of God's glory he wishes to give us.

One of the difficulties with the first is our tendency to exclude much of what goes on in everyday life from our worship. Occasionally perhaps this is deliberate, because we know that there are aspects of our life which will not bear God's examination, but much more often it is because we have not reflected sufficiently on how much of life there is to bring in. Individual concerns are brought; corporate or societal ones often are not, because they have never been formulated as concerns. That is partly because we have not taken seriously enough our need to be envisioned – to be *shown* what matters; we assume we know. So intercessory prayer, for example, concentrates on the illness, crisis and disaster which we can see needs putting right, with the tacit implication that we can manage the rest ourselves and do not need to be guided in what to ask for. The offertory, which in some eucharistic theology acts as a key focal point for our desire for trans-formation in the world's life, and our belief in the possibility of it, may become a rather formal 'bringing up the bread and wine'; in many non-eucharistic services, it becomes purely a thank-offering, which, important though that is, often leaves unasked and unanswered the question of what God wants to be given. The confession, which might at an earlier stage in the service have sensitized worshippers to this question, can be very formal indeed, and offer people little help in bringing to God the world's sins in which they are caught up as opposed to those which are their direct and sole responsibility. (Nor perhaps is it clear to many congregations what confessing sins on the world's behalf might mean, however much they might claim to believe in the priesthood of all believers.)

In all of this there is the marginalization of God's judgment, which Revelation so clearly presents as an essential part of encountering the Saviour God – and so salvation also becomes low-key, at least in the sense of what God has done for the world. Celebration of individuals' personal relationship with God through Christ may well take place, and is entirely appropriate – but it is often not matched by anything approaching the same celebration of how God's kingdom triumphs in the world, and the sense of God at work in the world remains undeveloped.

What can be done about all this? Worship leaders of course bear a major responsibility. Prophetic preaching can sharpen people's vision of the world and of God's judgment upon their place in it, though to be effective, judgmental preaching needs much humility on the part of the preacher, and a gospel remedy which people can follow in practice as well as a prophetic diagnosis. The words which people are offered to use in their prayers, whether thanksgiving, confession or intercession, can also be highly effective in helping people to see the world in God's light. But worship leaders need to recognize their own limitations. Large parts of the life experience even of many in their own congregations are a closed book to them (the working lives of worshippers in paid employment are one prime example for most worship leaders, not to mention the experience of those who differ from them in race or age or economic status); and that is before one begins on the experiences of those from other countries and cultures. This all needs to be brought into worship too.

Much may be done by the informed and careful choice of worship material, and in particular the regular use of material from the world church. But the resources of the local congregation are also to be used. People's individual prayers are important, especially if a corporate silence can unite those prayers. Not only does such a silence allow the whole body of worshippers to contribute to the range of the prayer, it may well be the prayer of greatest depth: if we are confronting the crying needs and crying evils of the world, we may need to be silent.[18] But more overt participation may help too, whether from individuals or from groups. Such contributions can be blessedly concrete, and so make the unfamiliar worlds come alive. Parents or teachers – or children or young people – might describe a local school as a preparation for prayers of thanksgiving and intercession; or a campaigning group might report on progress on a community or international issue; or a banner-making group explain its work on a particular theme. This is not just giving different groups their innings; it is helping the whole worshipping community to broaden its horizons as it brings to God the world of which it is a part.

If we succeed in bringing the world to God in our worship, then we have to ask secondly to whom are we bringing it, how we should prepare ourselves to meet him, and what, if anything, we expect him to do. If we learn from the vision of Revelation, we shall see ourselves as worshipping the sovereign God and the victorious Lamb. It is important to emphasize this, because the truths of God's sovereignty and Christ's victory are so little believed in the world from which worshippers come (at least in the West). There may still be relatively few convinced atheists in theory, but what might be called 'practical atheists' are many: on the whole people do not believe in a God whose writ runs. Nor do they believe in the efficacy of sacrifice: they may admire it, but on the whole they believe it is 'looking after number one' that works, and is the only practical basis for living. But it is not only the general disinterest and disbelief by which Christians are surrounded. There are also a great many people in the world whose perceived interest lies in maintaining the worship of society's false gods; and they tell insidiously powerful lies. People need to feed richly in worship on the truths about God and Christ if they are to withstand this, and so be enabled to live the worship of God in the world.

God does not need us to defend his sovereignty, he is his own interpreter, and he comes when he chooses: we cannot engineer a worship experience of his power and his glory. But no attention given to preparing ourselves is wasted, and we could perhaps learn better to treat him as sovereign in our worship, not only in thought and word about his will and our obedience, nor even in a more complete submitting of the world's life to his judgment, but in stillness and waiting. Perhaps it is the last which will make the most impression, for stillness and waiting are deeply countercultural things in today's Western world – the rich and powerful do not wait, and there is not much stillness either for those who must get or guard power and wealth. And we need to put ourselves in the way of encountering God in his sovereignty. This is not to deny the wonder of the closeness and intimacy of God in his fatherhood, and motherhood; but it is to prevent this becoming a cheap coziness. Truth and wonder alike are lost if instead of marvelling at God coming down to our level we cut him down to our size.

> And will this sovereign King
> Of glory condescend?
> And will he write his name
> My Father and my friend?[19]

Moreover, to return to Revelation's central concern, if God is not sovereign, why should we hope for victory?

Which leads us to the question of how we are to catch the vision of the victory of the Lamb. One of the gifts of charismatic worship has been to offer songs that worship Christ in the language of victory, for it has helped to re-establish his victory as a living reality in people's minds. But the criticism of 'triumphalism' is sometimes well-founded. There is not much in Revelation of mighty Christian armies sweeping across the land in the present age: more characteristic is 'I know that you have but little power, and yet you have kept my word and have not denied my name' (3.8). Conquering is resisting evil, where necessary at personal cost. We need therefore to express in our worship a sense of present struggle, and of victory that is hoped for and anticipated rather than fully realized. Perhaps it is the sense of ultimate victory that is key, for if there is no such victory, then people's sufferings remain simply sufferings, to be relieved if possible by the generosity of the better off; if victory is to come, then there is a struggle on, in which we are called to solidarity.

We are in need of theological teaching in this. There is in most mainstream churches very little preaching on the 'second coming' which is how we usually refer to the end of human history. Yet it is hard to believe that the first coming of Christ offers all the hope we need. Deeply sufficient though his followers over twenty centuries have proved his grace to be, we hope for more than evil endured and conquered in terms of personal faithfulness: the resurrection in which we believe means fullness of life for the whole world and we are still waiting for that. We need preachers and teachers to make the theology of the end come alive for us.

Not that we are without *signs* of resurrection. Perhaps one of the most effective ways of making real the prospect of God's ultimate victory is to celebrate the anticipatory triumphs of grace: the communities (within the church or outside it) where people succeed in living by the values of the new earth, the places where little victories are won over racism or exploitation, the times when profit is foregone or the truth is told by someone who will suffer for it, the people who are examples of integrity and compassion and endurance. The church, for all its faults, is a place of such victories, and a people which knows the source of them; we do well in worship to praise God for what he has done as well as belabour ourselves for what we have failed to do. We do well also to use the hymns and prayers, and share the thinking, of Christians other than ourselves who may have much more insight than we do into struggles against structural evil, and who may be calling us to be in solidarity with them in our prayers and thinking and action.

We are not in control in worship; nor do we know what God will do with our attempts to bring our life in the world more completely before him, and to submit it to the sovereign Lord who wins victories from a cross. But, if we believe

Revelation, we can humbly expect such worship to sharpen our vision. We may expect a clearer view of what we have to resist, a surer conviction of the triumph of goodness, and a growing realization that to be with the Lamb is all that matters. And we may expect increasingly to find that daily life is worship too.

7

Witness: Communicating the Vision

If worship is the category of first importance in Revelation, witness runs it a close second. The link between the two is not quite the one we might suppose. It is not so much that worship is what goes on in church (or in private prayers) while witness is what Christians do in the world; for, as we have seen, John sees daily life in terms of worship as well as church services. Rather, in Revelation, worship is giving worth to God (or in false worship to other people or things), while witness is communicating that sense of worth to other people. Worship is acknowledging the truth, in other words, and witness is telling it. And that telling is important because, as John sees it, it is part of God's salvation plan for the world.

Before looking at Revelation's particular understanding of the church's witness, it may be helpful to notice how important a category witness is in the New Testament view of things generally. We have already seen in chapter three that the first Christians expected the world as they knew it to end in their life-time, with the return of Christ in glory. In this understanding, the final bringing in of God's kingdom was to be prayed for rather than worked for: God would bring in his Day at his own time by his own power. There was nevertheless a profound responsibility laid upon the Christian community, and its apostles and prophets in particular: the world must be told about Christ, so that everyone would have the chance to believe in him and so find God's salvation. Hence the anxiety Paul reveals in the letter to the Romans to preach the gospel where it has not been heard;[1] hence the insistence of the

Gospel-writers that before the End: 'the good news must first be proclaimed to all nations';[2] hence, most familiarly, the description in Acts of the church's task as it waits for Christ's final coming:

> It is not for you to know times or periods that the Father has set by his own authority. But you will receive power when the Holy Spirit has come upon you; and *you will be my witnesses* in Jerusalem, and in all Judaea and Samaria, and to the ends of the earth (1.7–8).

Witness, in other words, is *the* task of the church as it awaits the End.

But what does witness mean? It is easy from the quotations above to suppose that witness is primarily a matter of 'preaching Christ', and certainly that has to be a central element in witness. But other New Testament passages suggest that we should take a wider view, not least those passages where the word 'witness' is used, not of Christians, but of Christ himself. One of these is in Revelation, where the phrase 'faithful witness' is in fact the first description for Christ; another is in I Timothy, where the writer speaks of 'Christ Jesus who in his testimony (witness) before Pontius Pilate made the good confession'.[3] While both these references doubtless include Jesus' own words about himself, and are thus a sort of 'preaching Christ', there is also in both a clear association with the fact of his death. We are being presented, in other words, with what soon becomes the dominant sense of 'witness', which is suffering for the truth in which you believe, if necessary to the point of death. (The Greek word for 'witness' is 'martyr'.) But the understanding of Christ as himself a witness to God suggests an even broader significance for the word. It must be the whole of what Christ was that is witness, and not just his words, nor even only his death; everything about him presents the world with the truth about God. But if that is so, then everything about Christians which communicates something truly Christ-like (and therefore true to God) will have that same essential nature of witness. Can this idea of witness help us see what Christians might be doing about the world's present predicament, and its future promise?

At this point we need to return to the problem situation we outlined in chapter one: many Christians want to live out their faith in the world but feel helpless in the face of world problems that are just too big to make any impression on. It is the argument of this book that Revelation's idea of witness would be very helpful here, and might be a better starting point than thinking that we must try to improve the world. This is not an open and shut argument, and to explain it we need briefly to look at ethical theory.

Though everybody with any moral sense at all does ethics in practice (that is, they have some idea of what is right and wrong and make at least some attempt to live by it), it is surprisingly difficult to explain why you think you should do some things and not do others. Basically there are two sorts of reasons, for which the technical terms are *consequential* and *deontological*. If you take a consequential approach, as the name suggests, you look at the likely results of what you are thinking of doing, and if they are on the whole good, or at least better than any other option, then you decide you should go ahead and do it. The most famous classical version of this is a theory called *utilitarianism* (rather confusingly, since it has little to do with what we mean by utility); according to this you should do what leads to the greatest happiness of the greatest number of people.[4] On the other hand, if you take a deontological approach, you do something because you feel for one reason or another that you 'must'[5] – the Bible says you should, or your parents brought you up to, or you just 'can't' do otherwise – and the results don't come into it. To give a trivial example, the consequentialist reply to 'do you like me in this hat?' (where the hat is a mistake) is 'yes, it's lovely'; the deontological reply from someone brought up to tell the truth at all costs is 'you look terrible'.

Consequentialists take a good deal of responsibility upon

themselves, more than some people think is wise or reasonable. They end up deciding what is really for everyone's good, and they also take on a great burden of responsibility for what other people will do. To take a very *un*trivial example, consequentialists are likely to feel that the rise in back-street abortions that will follow restrictive abortion laws are in some sense the responsibility of those who pass those laws, even though they will neither ask for nor perform the abortions that follow; and because of the suffering that will result, they will tend to think it right to keep the laws less restrictive. Deontologists, on the other hand, are likely to say that the taking of life that abortion represents is simply impermissible, and that the abortion law should reflect that truth as closely as possible. They will refuse to accept that they have a moral responsibility for the back-street abortions that follow a tighter law (because ultimately human beings must make their own decisions), though they will very probably accept the obligation to take steps to minimize the demand for them. Deontologists may also well ask the consequentialists why they are so sure that maximum well-being *is* secured by allowing large numbers of abortions. They will say that there is a clear responsibility to maintain the principle of not taking life, but that to ensure the 'happiest' results for everyone requires more wisdom and power than is ours, and is therefore not our responsibility; to assume that it is is a dangerous illusion.

Where issues of justice, peace and the care of the environment are concerned most people probably take the consequentialist approach. They want above all to do what will make things better – what will reduce the numbers of starving children, prevent the wars, stop the rain forests disappearing. It may therefore seem rather odd to argue, as this book does, for a 'witness' approach to these questions, since witness belongs on the deontological side of the fence.

It is not witnesses' responsibility to ask what the results of their witness will be; it is their responsibility to tell (or act on) the truth. Thus, when it comes to world issues, witnesses will not ask how effective a demonstration about world debt is going to be; they will demonstrate out of a sense of injustice, to give voice to what cries out to be heard. Witnesses will not boycott certain products in the expectation, or even in one sense the hope, that economic pressure will lead to the fall of an oppressive regime, or to a change of policy in a big company; they will boycott because they want to resist what they see to be contrary to God's desire for human well-being. Like all deontologists, they are interested in principles first, and results second.

Of course there is a perverse version of this. It is not hard to imagine witnesses on the Revelation model who become so concerned with their own faithfulness, or with the wickedness of those they are fighting, that they forget to ask what is happening to the people in whose interests the battle is supposed to be. That would be unattractive self-righteousness at best, and at worst dangerous fanaticism. Common sense, not to mention humanity, dictates *some* concern with results, and not to choose that form of witness which seemed likely to have most immediate effect would be merely silly. Consequential and deontological approaches to moral decision-making are probably not wholly separable even in theory, and they certainly are not separable in practice, as any reader will realize who tried to come up with a response about the hat which was both true and kind. But it *is* being proposed that we liberate ourselves from letting results be our *primary* motivation.

For one thing, a 'results' motivation will not be enough to keep us going. As we have already suggested, all but the bravest souls will decide that the odds are too heavily weighted against them; and even they will be hampered by the sense of their own powerlessness. Witness, by contrast, has the compulsion of worship about it. When we see the glory of God in heaven we bow down in awe and wonder – we have to. When we see what God wants for his children on earth we work, and if necessary fight for it – we have to. In both cases we are responding to the goodness of God. That is constant, and will constantly be there to evoke our response.

Another problem about working on a 'results' basis is that, when it comes to global issues, results are not at all easy to see. Who would hazard a judgment, even with hindsight, as to how far demonstrations against apartheid, or even the boycott of South African goods, contributed to apartheid's fall? To witness to what you see to be the truth of God's values will often be a much more certain guide to action than to go for what will 'work'. And, perhaps most fundamentally of all, it will acknowledge that God is at work in the world where a 'results' motivation is in danger of sidelining him.

For where it is the results which *we* can see and measure which count, we are within an ace of thinking that it is we who are doing it all, which is a total denial of a God who is active in the world. To use the analogy of the play we quoted in chapter four, it may well be that God 'has no hands but our hands', in the sense that he has chosen to let us be the actors, even actors with a large measure of direction, but that is very different from saying that God is not influencing the play, or is unable to bring it to his own conclusion. Revelation, as we have seen, is very reticent about *how* God uses faithful witness in the establishing of his kingdom, but it is crystal clear *that* he does so. We are invited to share that confidence in the results that God will bring. While of course if we are human at all we care about the results we see, or agonizingly fail to see, on the way, we have nevertheless to give our first attention to ensuring that we are faithful witnesses.

Witness, as we have said, is a sense of what is true, *communicated* to others, and it is now time to see how Revelation envisages this as happening. The primary passage about witness is worth quoting in full:

'And I will grant my two witnesses authority to prophesy for one thousand two hundred and sixty days, wearing sackcloth.' These are the two olive trees and the two lampstands that stand before the Lord of the earth. And if anyone wants to harm them, fire pours from their mouth and consumes their foes; anyone who wants to harm them must be killed in this manner. They have authority to shut the sky, so that no rain may fall during the days of their prophesying, and they have authority over the waters to turn them into blood, and to strike the earth with every kind of plague, as often as they desire. When they have finished their testimony, the beast that comes up from the bottomless pit will make war on them and conquer them and kill them, and their dead bodies will lie in the street of the great city that is prophetically called Sodom and Egypt, where also their Lord was crucified. For three and a half days members of the peoples and tribes and languages and nations will gaze at their dead bodies and refuse to let them be placed in a tomb; and the inhabitants of the earth will gloat over them and celebrate and exchange presents, because these two prophets had been a torment to the inhabitants of the earth. But after the three and a half days, the breath of life from God entered them, and they stood on their feet, and those who saw them were terrified. Then they heard a loud voice from heaven saying to them, 'Come up here!' And they went up to heaven in a cloud while their enemies watched them. At that moment there was a great earthquake, and a tenth of the city fell; seven thousand people were killed in the earthquake, and the rest were terrified and gave glory to the God of heaven (11.3–13).

There are several remarkable things about this passage, which appears to be a recapitulation of all the prophetic witness of the past (Elijah and Moses being particularly obvious); this culminates in a final vindication of the prophets, who at that point stand (probably) for the Christian church as prophetic community.[6] Immediately striking are the contrasts between the very different situations of the witnesses at various stages in the story. They move from being all-powerful and victorious (though, curiously, clothed in sackcloth as they prophesy), through utter defeat and death, to ultimate vindication through resurrection and ascension; in all this they are obviously following the pattern discernible in

Jesus' own story. Less immediately noteworthy, but quite crucially significant, is the response to the earthquake at the end of the passage: after the death of the seven thousand, 'the rest were terrified and gave glory to the God of heaven'. It is tempting for the casual reader to respond by saying, 'well they would, wouldn't they?', but in fact this is a quite unusual response in Revelation; normally people respond to judgment disasters by cursing and going on sinning. The irresistible conclusion is that it is the prophetic witness combined with the disaster which has elicited the repentance.

Here then is the 'place in the story' of God's saving work in the world for the saints to take up. It is for them to interpret to people the disasters which are happening as the judgments of God, which are not simply inevitable, but are meant to lead to a change of heart. John makes no attempt to say how successful the prophetic community may be in this; he certainly does not envisage a total success story, for failures to repent follow chapter eleven just as they precede it, but the possibility of others taking notice of what the prophetic community has seen and is prepared to tell is clearly signalled. Witness is communicating the vision, and inviting a response to it.

The vision we have to communicate, as Revelation sees it, is two-sided. For the world, we have a vision of what it could (and we believe will) be, a clear-sighted appreciation of what it now is, and a picture of how, given our starting point, the End may be reached (chapter five). On the other side, we have a vision of the God who has created and redeemed that world, sovereign and victorious, but winning his victories by truth and love, and not by force (chapter six). If we are to communicate that vision to those who have not yet been grasped by it, where do we start?

The passage about the witnesses which we have quoted would indicate starting with the world in its present state: the prophets sitting in sackcloth, and obviously making themselves extremely unpopular with people, suggest a scenario of trenchant denunciation of the present world's ills. And in one sense the present state of things is the obvious place to start.

'What's wrong with the world' is, at one level or another, a constant topic of interest to people, and, if we have at all taken on board the obligation upon the church to be a prophetic community, we have both a diagnosis and a warning about what is wrong which we ought to be offering to people. To put it in traditional Christian language, the world's ills are due to sin, sin is destructive, is bound to be destructive, and the only way out of it is repentance. But how many Christians would want to say that?

Let us put the difficulty in as controversial a form as possible. The AIDS epidemic, which is such grief for individuals and for whole nations, has spread as it has because people have not confined their sexual relationships to one partner in the way that traditional Christian morality prescribes. Our reading of Revelation has understood God's wrath as meaning essentially that sin has consequences which are destructive, of the innocent as well as of the guilty; and on this understanding AIDS is an obvious example of that wrath. Do we then wish our church leaders to go on television and proclaim that AIDS is the wrath of God? Would we support them in the lively conversations that would doubtless follow among those who had watched the programme?

For many Christians the answer to those questions would be 'no', probably on one or more of the following grounds:

'Our God isn't an angry God who enjoys punishing people';

'People with AIDS need loving, not blaming';

'It won't do any good; people think the church is always going on about sex, and it will only put their backs up' (or, more simply, 'goodness, I wouldn't dare say that').

The first of these objections is the most compelling. Although the wrath of God does not on our understanding mean that God is an angry punisher of sinners, probably even most Christians think it does, and it is highly likely that most other people will. Those who cannot make themselves understood are not a great success as witnesses, and the church leaders in this example would accordingly be wise to avoid 'wrath of God' language.

But even it if is expressed differently, the idea will still be offensive (the third objection). The wrath of God *does* mean that God has certain intentions for human behaviour (including sexual behaviour), and that if they are ignored trouble and suffering inevitably follow. This is more than saying that 'unsafe' sex is dangerous and irresponsible, although it certainly includes that message; it is saying that sex outside the limits which God has set is dangerous because it is wrong. That will be a deeply unpopular message, partly because people want a much higher degree of sexual freedom than Christian teaching allows, and partly because people do not like being told they are wrong. Does it matter if people are offended in this way?

Honesty compels us to say that it will matter to us. Offended people are hostile people, and hostility is not easy to bear. (It is easier to say that other people should speak out than to do so oneself.) Being a Christian does not mean that one is not prone to self-deception, and we need therefore to be aware that what masquerades as concern that other people should not be put off is often in fact concern that we should not get hurt. But, acknowledging our own possible cowardice in the matter, will it in fact do any good loudly to proclaim that certain kinds of sexual behaviour are wrong? Will not church leaders pontificating on the subject simply be ignored? Or, if they are not, may they not do positive damage, either by provoking a counterproductive anger in those they criticize, or, to stay with the AIDS example, by encouraging a lack of sympathy for extremely vulnerable people? Here lies much of the force of the second objection, that Christians should love, not blame.

To ask about the good or bad results of criticizing behaviour as dangerous and wrong is of course a consequentialist question, and witnesses might simply reply that it is their business to tell the truth, not to do what looks likely to produce the greatest happiness (or least unhappiness). But they might be more convincing if they justified their truth-telling at least partly in terms of its results, for few of us think that results are totally to be ignored. So, given the undoubted offence and unhappiness that truthful witness will sometimes cause, can the witness advance any counterarguments about the good that truth-telling does?

One such argument is that, unless we are prepared to label some behaviour as wrong, we shall not be able to talk about right behaviour. But if we never expound the Christian moral tradition (about sexual behaviour or anything else), we deprive people of a body of wisdom about how to live that they badly need. For all we may say about people's freedom and their ultimate responsibility to make their own moral decisions, nobody makes those decisions uninfluenced by others, and we need to be taught principles of behaviour. Children who have been brought up 'not knowing the difference between right and wrong' are greatly to be pitied, and adults who have not internalized rules of behaviour which they sometimes impose upon themselves against their own desire are monsters. The law of God is about how to live well; rightly understood, it is a great gift, and one to be shared with people.

Secondly, if people are never wrong, there is not much gospel left. Forgiveness, which is at the heart of the gospel, only makes sense if there is something to forgive. If the truth is, as we believe, that the road to a better world is by acknowledging wrong and by the grace of God turning one's back upon it, there is no way out of naming the wrong, however uncomfortable for ourselves or for others. Gospel as well as law, in other words, requires that we witness to what is wrong with the world. We owe the world the truth, and though we should never be gratuitously offensive, we cannot suppress the truth just because it may offend.

Thus if those who object that 'people need loving, not blaming' are saying that it is lacking in compassion to label certain behaviour as wrong, they are making a serious mistake: it is leaving people *un*warned about behaviour that will harm them and others which is lacking in compassion. Nevertheless the objection is making a very serious point. It is particularly important in the AIDS example we have been working with, but it applies across the board. Criticism of people's behaviour which condemns the people themselves cannot be an authentic Christian witness. Many people in fact think that you cannot have one without the other, and that a claim to 'hate the sin but love the sinner' is simply hypocritical. They may overestimate the difficulties (it seems fairly simple to do for oneself, as C. S. Lewis once remarked);[7] but it is certainly not easy to label other people's behaviour as wrong without being judgmental about them, and perhaps encouraging a judgmental attitude elsewhere. Witnesses to the world's wrongs will inevitably be accused of smug self-righteousness, and they have to ask themselves whether the accusations are true. They have also to make it crystal clear that to judge the ultimate guilt of anyone is God's business and not ours, and that our obligation to care for those who need care in any case depends not one jot upon their guilt or innocence – for what is the gospel if not the fact that the guilty are precious to God? This aspect of witness will require action, and not just words.

This is the point at which it is important to look again at the witnesses *in sackcloth*, that is, identified with the sinners they are criticizing and not set over against them. For anyone thinking about witness on the basis of Revelation will realize that Christians are not safely free of the world's wrongs, and that they are therefore in no position to take a lofty and superior attitude towards others. Our witness will be most authentic in Revelation's terms when we name the wrongs of which *we* are guilty as well as the 'world', and attempt to find, and show, the repentant way out of them. The criticism of a sexual promiscuity that is not on the whole characteristic of the church may be necessary and right, but Revelation would suggest going first for sins nearer home – and for putting one's own house in order before criticizing others. It is 'worldly' behaviour *in the church* that John wants most passionately to combat. Most Christians are glad to see the churches pressing governments to remit the debt of poor countries; John would be asking why rich congregations corner resources for them-

selves while poor congregations down the road struggle to
keep going. Christians join in pressing the police to root out
institutional racism; John would be asking what the churches
are doing to root out their own. We do not have to have solved
all the problems of injustice and lack of peace within our
own life (we are probably more use as examples of people
struggling with them); but integrity requires that we recognize
our own shortcomings and try to turn our backs on them.
And, to return to our concern with results, effectiveness as
witnesses requires the same. Critics who know nothing of the
behaviour which they are criticizing are seldom listened to.[8]
Nor are those who are happily behaving in the same way
themselves. Witnesses do not have to be popular, but they do
have to be credible.

In speaking of *repentant* witnesses we have made an
important move. In much of the discussion so far we have
been talking as if witnessing equalled explaining to people
what was wrong with the world. We have spent time on this
issue, because so many present-day Western Christians
find difficulty with it. But in fact, as we have already said,
explaining what is wrong with things is only the beginning of
what we have to communicate, and we should be seriously
misleading witnesses if we had nothing positive to affirm.
Repentance is the beginning of the positive, though perhaps it
does not sound so to those who think of it as merely breast-
beating. Rightly understood as a turning round, repentance
for the reader of Revelation is an opening of oneself to hope
for the world, to a vision of what the world could and will be,
and to a present life lived in the light of that vision, lived by
'End' values. And all this is grounded in a vision of God and of
the Lamb, not only of their glory but of their love for the
world. That above all is to be witnessed to.

Communicating so inclusive a vision will be a matter of
much more than words; it will be all that we do and are. Some
of what this means will be discussed in our final chapter, but it
will be appropriate here to end with some general comments
on the positive side of our witness.

We have outlined in chapter five (pp. 71ff., 83) the positive values which we can derive from Revelation's vision of the new earth. Some of the values in which Christians believe and for which they work are shared by others, and it is important with a text like Revelation, which is so often strongly counter-cultural, to emphasize that witness does not necessarily mean being alone against the world. There are many people of other faiths or of no faith whose commitment to human well-being on a basis of inclusiveness, and to the care of the environment, match, or indeed surpass, the commitment of Christians; and Christians should be grateful for partnership with them when that is appropriate. But there will be cases when the understanding of human well-being as reflecting the intentions of a sovereign creator will give Christians something distinctive to say which may not be shared, say, by those with a humanist commitment. Of the many possible arguments against cloning, for example, only believers in a creator are going to say, 'but God doesn't go in for exact copies'. And sometimes basic Christian values will be contrary to the prevailing climate of opinion. The value for community over against individual freedom is one example, and the value placed on sacrifice over against self-fulfilment is another.

Witness here is not only communicating our vision of how the world could and should be, and how we should act in it. Because all the values that we commend in such witness in the end depend on the kind of God we believe in, we shall also be witnessing in the narrower and more central sense of communicating the truths of God as we have been given to know him. Many of the things we shall want to say about our use of the earth's resources will depend on the fact that they are gifts entrusted to us by a sovereign creator. Many of our attitudes to technology and our use of it will depend on our view of human beings as made in God's image yet not meant to snatch at equality with him. Much of what we shall say and work for in the way human beings are treated will depend on God's self-revelation in Christ as the friend of the undeserving and the unregarded. Christians who engage with the issues of the world have a wealth of possibilities of explaining and commending the Saviour in whom they believe.[9]

If this is true as we try to share the values we have for our world, it is if anything even more true as we share our convictions about how our vision is to be realized. For here we depend wholly on God's being the God whom Revelation shows us, a God with the Lamb at his heart. That God is to be preached, and spoken about, but for many who will not listen, the most effective witness will be the quality of Christians' lives. There will be about people who believe in a sovereign God whose will cannot ultimately be thwarted a persistent hopefulness about their witness that an often cynical world very badly needs. There will be about people who believe in a slaughtered, standing Lamb a persistent graciousness in loving that can make people hopeful, even about themselves. And these witnesses will know how to stand for what they believe, and to suffer if need be for what they believe. They will not ask too many questions about what effect they are having. But they must have a place in the story of God in the world.

8

Following the Lamb

Revelation has a large vision for small churches. The church lives in the world, and it has a part to play in the history of the world. Whether or not it plays that part depends essentially on its faithfulness: will it follow the Lamb? Our final chapter will ask what following the Lamb might mean for Christians today.

We have first to recognize that Revelation's concern is over-whelmingly with Christian communities rather than with individuals. That cannot mean that individual commitment to the way of Jesus is unimportant, for there are clearly demands made of Christians in the book that only individuals can take upon themselves, and honour. It is individuals who make many of the 'worship' decisions in life, choosing those things to which they will give ultimate value, and the sacrifices they will make for the sake of what is worshipped. It is individuals who in large measure make 'witness' decisions, in terms of what they are prepared to say and do as Christians in the world, and at what cost to themselves. There will be no following of the Lamb without individual commitment. Yet even the decisions that we count most personal are more influenced than we may sometimes recognize by the values and practices that our community has taken as its own. Other people help us see what is truly valuable and they support and encourage us in witnessing to our values. Even more clearly we depend on the community for the basic understandings of God and the world which underpin our worship and witness. So, perhaps as a helpful corrective in an over-individualist age, and certainly in line with Revelation's concern, we shall concentrate in this final chapter on asking what it might mean for Christian communities to follow the Lamb.

If we have learnt anything from this visionary book, we shall understand that one of the most crucial questions will be how these communities *see* things. We have looked in earlier chapters at how Revelation invites us to look at the world, and at God, but now it may be helpful to recapitulate some of what we have said by asking how Christian communities are to look at themselves. As the letters to the churches make clear, Revelation has a strong sense of Christian communities as having a corporate identity; we are not talking about abstractions but about real entities, with material 'outsides' and spiritual 'insides', to use the language of our third chapter.

Before proceeding, perhaps we should address the question of what we mean by 'the churches'. Are we talking just about congregations? If so, many readers (though not all) may feel this to be a very inadequate way of looking at the Church with a capital 'C' and its relationship with the world. They may indeed be confirmed in a suspicion which arises on other grounds that Revelation is a sectarian book, chiefly interested in preserving the purity of holy huddles. We have suggested in chapter three that John in choosing to write to seven churches has a more catholic understanding of 'church' than that, though he undoubtedly has a strong sense of the importance of the local congregation as well as of the Church as a whole. Perhaps that combination of understandings is a helpful pointer to follow. Christians relate to their fellow-Christians at a number of different levels: in a small group, a congregation, a denomination, or in the universal Church, to name only some. And they relate to the world in different ways from within each of these communities, ways which are determined both by the spiritual 'insides' of these communities and their institutional 'outsides'. So the question about how the church sees itself may relate to a number of settings.[1]

The first truth for the church (at any level) to recognize is that it is in the world. That means responsibility, for as we have seen in chapter seven the church has the role of prophetic witness to the world; but it also clearly, in John's eyes, means danger, for the church may be corrupted by the world, and led by it into false worship, whether of money, power or status. It has to be recognized that it is hard to hold these two insights in balance. To take seriously the church's mission responsibility in the world is to get involved, to get alongside, not to be judgmental; to take seriously the danger of the world is to be critical, and at least to some degree to be separate. Can we do both at once? Should we?

The instinct of many Christians will be to say 'no' to the latter question. We should forget the critical and the separate and go for the mission involvement. What is Christ about if not about getting alongside, getting his hands dirty? But are we strong enough to do that and maintain our own Christian position, or shall we find, to use the trenchant words of a book on the contemporary church, that in leaning over to talk to the world, we have fallen in?[2] Even Christ had his separateness, and not only the separateness of his solitary prayer with the Father, but the separateness of his own small community to whom he was not afraid to say, 'this is how the world does it, but "it is not so among you"'.[3] Is the church today as different from the world as Christ would want in its attitude to money, or to status? And if it is not, is that not in large measure because the church has not seen how dangerously powerful the world is in infecting the church with its own God-less values? The church is in the world, and its people are exposed to precisely the same powers as everyone else.

And yet those who fear sectarianism have to be listened to. To take seriously the danger of the world has the obvious temptation to separate oneself and concentrate on one's own holiness (or perhaps just one's own coziness and comfort), with the mission of the church nowhere. Such indifference to others on the one hand and self-concern, and very probably self-righteousness, on the other are equally contrary to the gospel. Revelation, it must be admitted, is not nearly as clear in its warning of these dangers as it is of the dangers of being 'conformed to this world', as Paul would put it.[4] Nevertheless, if we have been right in highlighting the book's concern with the world's ultimate well-being and the role that it sees for the saints in God's bringing about that well-being, we can read in Revelation the call to be in the world to some purpose, as well as to be 'in the world but not of the world'.[5]

An improper sectarianism will be held in check by discernment. We saw in chapter three that the most helpful way to use the imagery of the beast was not simplistically to label people or institutions as beasts, but to ask whether they are beastly, and if they are, then in what respects and on what occasions. A church which takes Revelation seriously is not asked to be totally world-denying; indeed it is asked in so far as it sees life in terms of struggle to affirm and support what is of God and of the Lamb (consciously or otherwise) with the same enthusiasm that it brings to resisting what is opposed to them. But it *is* asked to be critical of the world in which it finds itself; or else it will not be able to discern what is in God's sight life-denying, or turn its back upon it, or invite the world to turn its back upon it. And it may then find itself offering (to itself and others) the false gospel which short-cuts repentance, and invites people to feel good about going on sinning. Such a gospel leaves the world defenceless in the face of the wrath of God.

Seeing and telling what is wrong is clearly not a soft option, but it is not the self-righteous gloom and doom that it is often accused of being (sometimes with justification); rather it is the beginning of the road to life. The church does not find repentance easy, but it knows that it is not another word for wallowing in guilt; it is what puts people in touch with the one who 'loves us and freed us from our sins' (1.5b) and so makes a new life possible. Where the church believes and practises that gospel, it has an inevitable separateness from the world, but the separateness, like Christ's own, is entirely at the world's service, for the gospel is to be offered to the world.[6] We have spoken as if separateness and mission were polar opposites, and in practice they may often present the church with a difficult balancing act, but essentially what preserves the church's distinctiveness is what ensures that its mission is real.

The church which sees itself in the world and with a gospel for the world will be a repentant community. If it takes seriously its own susceptibility to the world's evils, it will not just criticize the world for being materialistic, it will examine itself for an improper concern with money and things. It will not only decry the division of the world into 'haves' and 'have nots', but will ask what it can do to redress the imbalances between rich and poor congregations, or, in world terms, between churches in rich and poor countries. It will not only lament the racism in society, but will seek to become aware of and turn its back upon its own racism. It will not only oppose the cruelties of dictators or criticize the shenanigans of politicians; it will be alert to its own abuses of power and failures to tell the truth. How can the church do all this?

Bringing people to repentance is a prophetic task, and one of the church's problems today is a shortage of prophets. It is very noticeable in the New Testament church that leadership functions were divided between different people:

The gifts he gave were that some would be apostles, some prophets, some evangelists, some pastors and teachers . . .[7]

Mainstream churches today, on the other hand, expect their ordained leaders to be most, if not all, of these at once, and the inevitable consequence is that prophecy gets short-changed. For there are times when prophetic and pastoral roles are genuinely in conflict. How, for example, can someone who has on Saturday been sharing in the agonizing complexities of a failing marriage get into the pulpit on Sunday and preach to the same person a hard-hitting sermon about the damage done to children by divorce? Quite understandably the sermon is shelved in the name of pastoral sensitivity. But then an opportunity to present people with what God wants for human families has been lost.

This example highlights other difficulties with being prophetic. In the many-sided question of divorce, who is to say that more damage is *always* done to the children of a couple who divorce than if they had not done so? Nearly all the world issues with which this book is urging the church to get involved are highly complex ones, and sometimes expertise of quite a high order is required to understand them. Issues of the world economy are one example, and the enormous advances that are being made in the field of genetic engineering are another. Will not 'prophecy', which characteristically makes broad-brush and forceful statements, tend to be ludicrously simplistic, and thus bring the church into disrepute? And, since the issues are often highly dis- putable, will not pronouncements from on high about them be hopelessly divisive? Again we ask of church leaders what they cannot be expected to deliver. How can a bishop *both* be the focus of unity *and* 'speak out' on thoroughly contentious issues?

Prophets in every age have to consider what form their prophesying should take. They cannot guarantee a hearing, for they characteristically say what people do not much want to hear; but since their whole *raison d'être* is to convey God's truth, they have an obligation to be both credible and comprehensible. If issues are complex, then they must be pronounced on by people who are technically and theologic- ally qualified to understand the complexity; this suggests the high-powered working party (surely on an ecumenical basis) – perhaps with somebody else charged with the task of present- ing their conclusions in non-technical terms. But will the high- powered working party be prophetic? Perhaps that depends on the church's expectations. The working party is not to be asked for a spuriously objective presentation of the issues (one can be fair in examining ethical questions, but not neutral); it is to be asked to discern the word of the Lord. The pastors and teachers who share the working party's conclusions with local congregations are not just to explain them, but to invite people to respond appropriately. At the heart of the prophetic task of seeing and telling is the concern to know the will of God and do it; if that concern is there, then progress can be made, even if simple certainties cannot be offered, and obedient responses have to be provisional in the hope of further light being shed.

But sometimes the truth *is* simple and certain, and the prophetic task is to get it across. Since prophesying essentially entails envisioning, pictures may well take the place of words; visual images of how our world is suffering from our comfortable greed may speak volumes, and there are ever-increasing possibilities of presenting people with such images.[8] But words, and simple, proclamatory words at that, are not to be despised. With all the complexities of the issues that confront the world, the values that will drive our responses to its predicament can be very simply expressed: life is a gift, and it does not consist in the abundance of our possessions; God cares for the least and lowest, and is no respecter of persons; we cannot do anything ultimately against the truth, so we are not to lie; grace is stronger than sin, so we are not to despair. We need to say these things to each other, and we need the people, whatever we call them, who persist in telling us what these truths might mean for us in terms of concrete action and reaction to particular issues. If we do not have prophets, in other words, at least we should try to honour the prophetic. Of course not all who speak loudly and often are prophets, but sometimes people speak loudly and often because they are not being heard. The church needs both openness and discernment as it seeks to hear the prophetic voice.

But above all the church needs to act upon the truths it knows. For in the end, the repentant community is a community which turns round and starts acting differently. Perhaps one of the most urgent requirements of those who prophesy is that they should give people a clear way out of what is wrong. Denunciation which leaves people feeling guilty and powerless to do anything about it is worse than useless; like most attacks, it either leaves people flattened or hardens their resistance. Here is the place for the community which commits itself to a policy of response to world issues, not in an orgy of political correctness that leaves doubters, if not out, at least with their heads firmly down, but in a common acknowledgment that the followers of the Lamb must have something to say to, and do in, the world. Such a response might take various forms, depending on the nature and level of the community involved.

It is essential that the response be in action as well as in word. Not that talking is always an excuse for doing nothing, for sometimes we need to talk even to become aware that there is an issue, and sometimes we genuinely need to discuss quite carefully what action is appropriate. But we are not meant just to talk. There will be some issues on which a community will engage in active campaigning. This will be easiest where consciousness of the issues is already well-established and relatively uncontroversial: the Jubilee 2000 campaign has shown that, where there is little danger of damaging their own unity, the churches are beginning to fight less shy of political action than they have traditionally been. But it is important that the more controversial and less familiar issues are not simply avoided, for they are unlikely to be the least urgent. There may be specific issues where active involvement is confined to only some of the community's members, with the rest giving their moral support. Solidarity of this kind is not to be despised, any more than it is when a community is powerless to act directly, either through circumstance or because it simply has too much else to do. One of the commonest guilt traps is to do nothing because one cannot do everything; limited action, and solidarity where possible elsewhere, is a more constructive option. Such solidarity is fed by, and expressed in, prayer, which is not a cop-out: it is hard work if it is seriously engaged in, and is often valued by those prayed for in a way that surprises those who feel they are 'doing nothing about it'.

Prayer is essential also in sustaining what is perhaps the most important response to the world, that of openness to the sensitive issues. Sooner or later will arise the issues which impinge on our own life-style, or, even worse, require us to judge ourselves. The racism which infects much of the church is an example of such an issue which has been partly faced, but not adequately so. The issue of our involvement in the world economic system is one that has scarcely been addressed at all by most Western Christians. This may be understandable, for it affects the financial position of the church and everyone in it, and as we saw in chapter six it leaves many people open to the charge of idolatry; it is also extremely complex. But the church does need to engage with the important work on the subject which has now begun (of which Duchrow's *Alternatives to Global Capitalism* is a prime example).[9] For how can we shelve the issue which denies fullness of life to so many millions, without denying the lordship of God and his Christ over this world? If we will not face the hard issues, we are betraying a lack of commitment to what God wants for his world, or a lack of trust in his ability to bring it about. In Revelation's language, that is unfaithfulness, staining the clothes which have been washed in the blood of the Lamb.

A prophetic church that is challenging the world and making its own repentant witness is not only a church which sees itself as being in the world, but one which sees itself as figuring in the story of what God is doing there. There is a place for celebrating and affirming and offering to the world what the church is and does in its faithful following of the Lamb, as well as repentance for its imperfections. John's letters to the churches, for all their trenchant criticisms, are not afraid to praise, and they encourage Christian communities to 'hold fast to what you have'. For all its capacity for pettiness, the church is still the place of the big vision, and that is to be held on to. For all its real and shameful failures to be inclusive, still barriers of race and class and age and culture are crossed in the church in a way unparalleled by most human institutions. (Have we begun to realize the potential of the world-wide church as a body through which we can understand and relate to our global village?) Selfish as Christians can undoubtedly be, corporately as well as individually, there is a long and honoured tradition of giving and of care, not least to those who cannot (apparently) give much in return. Greedy and exploitative of the natural world as Christians have undoubtedly been, there is a tradition of Christian stewardship and of restraint in consumption that is of genuine relevance to today's needs. And all this is important, not so that Christians can give themselves a few pluses to offset the minuses, far less so that the church can look respectable in the eyes of the world; it is important because it is evidence of God at work among his people. That conviction is at the root of the hope that is in us, and it is that conviction which is ultimately what we have to offer to the world.

For the truth is that righteousness is not our project. Much as we may long for it, and much as we are called to work for it, as Revelation sees things, it is not in our hands. And so, paradoxically for a book which tells us of what must happen 'soon', Revelation frees us to take the long view. We shall grieve when what is right or true is denied, but we shall not be shaken in our conviction of its rightness or truth, nor doubt that one day it will prevail. We shall cry out, 'how long?' at the world's injustice, and the more we make the suffering it causes our own the more deeply felt the cry will be; but we shall not think that endurance and struggle are hopeless, for there will be an end to injustice. We shall, no doubt, be angry and frustrated with those who seem to us to be blind to the world's evil, or colluding with it; but we shall not fundamentally despair of them, for the slaughtered Lamb still stands, as he stands ready to forgive our own blindness and our own collusion. We may be personally hurt, and sad, when we fail in our attempts to improve things, and God will not discount or ignore our hurt and sadness; but our success or failure does not affect the final outcome.

This belief in the ability of God to change things is not just encouragement for ourselves, but the element in our witness which the world perhaps most needs to hear. Our commitment to a just and peaceful world in which the natural environment is cared for and respected is shared by many people of goodwill, some of whom put Christians to shame in what they do and bear in fighting for their beliefs. But people need hope if they are to persevere, and our present age, though in one sense one of much confidence in what humanity can do in the world, has also much doubt and fear about what humanity may do. A confidence in an absolute and ultimately victorious goodness at work in the world will be one of the greatest contributions that Christians can make to the struggle for the world's well-being.

But are we right to end on this note of assurance? For the world, Revelation clearly says yes. It is, through much tribulation, coming to a good end, for it will be made new. But for the church? On the one hand yes, all is assurance: Christians' weakness does not matter, their suffering will come to an end, the good that they long for they will see; they will share in the vindication and the glory of the Lamb. But . . . only if they follow the Lamb, and following the Lamb is hard. What is easy is for love to grow cold and apathy to set in, what is easy is to collude with convenient untruths and the world's false worship, what is easy is to look good on the outside and be dead on the inside. Faithfulness, on the other hand, is holding on when it is easier to let go, and it will mean, often, looking foolish and ineffective, arousing opposition, perhaps downright persecution. But only the faithful retain their place in the book of life.

So perhaps it is more true to Revelation to end with a question mark. Where in this story of God in the world do we appear?

Or with a different assurance:

I reprove and discipline those whom I love. Be earnest, therefore, and repent. Listen, I am standing at the door, knocking (3.19–20a).

Notes

1 *The Challenge of the New Millennium*

1. Figures from *Human Development Report 1999*, published for the United Nations Development Programme by OUP.
2. See *The Paradox of Prosperity*, Henley Centre/Salvation Army 1999, p. 14.
3. Todd Sandler, *Global Challenges: an Approach to Environmental, Political and Economic Problems*, CUP 1997.
4. President Ronald Reagan's description for the USSR.
5. Rex Ambler, *Global Theology: the Meaning of Faith in the Present World Crisis*, SCM Press 1990, p. 68.
6. Allan A. Boesak, *Comfort and Protest: Reflections on the Apocalypse of John on Patmos*, Saint Andrew Press 1987. For the historical influence of Revelation on the radical Christian tradition, see Christopher Rowland, *Radical Christianity*, Polity Press 1988, pp.82ff. and *passim*.
7. Hans Küng and Karl-Josef Kuschel (eds), *A Global Ethic*, ET SCM Press 1993.

2 *What is Revelation about?*

1. A. Yarbro Collins, *The Combat Myth in the Book of Revelation*, Scholars Press 1976, p.8.
2. There is also a good deal of what is technically called 'audition' in Revelation – John frequently says 'I heard' as well as 'I saw'; but we shall use the more ordinary word 'vision' to cover both kinds of experience.
3. The 'in the Spirit' references are 1.10, 4.2, 17.3 and 21.10.
4. 6.12ff., cf. Mark 13.24.
5. Cf. Ezek. 2.9–3.3.
6. See ch. 7, n. 6 (p. 140).

7. It would be mistaken to look for a single answer to the question of whom the woman represents, because the language of the chapter, as well as John's sophisticated use of allusion in general, suggests that several images are being used. There is Eve, 'the mother of all living', whose seed will bruise the serpent's head (Gen. 3.15); there is faithful Israel, sometimes conceived of as Yahweh's bride, from whom the Messiah will come; there is Mary, the mother of Jesus; and there is the church thought of as the mother of Christians. In and through Christ we are nurtured by all of these. For Satan's falling from heaven, cf. Luke 10.18, a verse today's readers often slide over.

8. For a question mark over whether the wine-harvest stands for unrelieved judgment, see below, ch. 4, pp. 50f.

9. See below, ch. 6, n. 11 (p. 139).

10. II Cor. 11.28.

11. W. M. Ramsay, *The Letters to the Seven Churches of Asia and their Place in the Plan of the Apocalypse*, Hodder and Stoughton 1904, pp.413–30.

12. Ramsay, *Letters*, pp. 185–96.

13. See 1.3, 22.18–19.

14. On church order, not only is it unclear how this developed among first century churches, nor how uniformly, but the date of Revelation is not agreed among scholars. See below, ch. 3, p. 45, and ch. 4, n. 4 (p. 135).

15. See, e.g., 1.9. Even the angels are not hierarchically-minded in Revelation: see, e.g., 22.9.

16. I Cor. 12.28.

17. See below ch. 7, pp. 109ff. This book's reading of Revelation in this area is heavily indebted to Richard Bauckham, *Climax of Prophecy: Studies on the Book of Revelation*, T & T Clark 1993, and also to F. D. Mazzaferri, *The Genre of the Book of Revelation from a Source-Critical Perspective*, de Gruyter, Berlin 1989.

18. Ezek. 2.3–3.3.

19. There is some evidence for the existence of scrolls used for legal documents that can be read a bit at a time, but no evidence that they were sealed at the end of each section. See Bauckham, *Climax of Prophecy*, p. 250.

20. Ezek. 1.4–28.

21. See 19.15, and cf. the initial vision of Christ (1.16), and the warning to the church in Pergamum (2.16).

22. Philadelphia is the only one of the seven churches not to be told to repent.

23. See, e.g., 9.20–21, 16.8, 16.21; the exception is 11.13, discussed in ch. 7 (pp. 110f.).

24. For the Lamb's army, see 14.1, which has a reference to 7.4ff.; for the saints' suffering resistance see, e.g., 6.9–11, 12.17, 13.7, and cf. the letter to the church in Smyrna at 2.10; and for the saints as witnesses bringing others to repentance, see below ch. 7, pp. 109ff.

25. 14.4. This is a difficult verse in its description of the Lamb's followers as those 'who have not defiled themselves with women, for they are virgins'. The image comes primarily from a military (quasi-ritual) context. War being conceived of as holy, sexual intercourse was thought to be a disqualification for military service; hence virginity here is part of the picture of the saints as the Lamb's army. In John's mind also is no doubt the general prophetic image of unfaithfulness to God as harlotry, made use of heavily in Revelation in the description of Babylon as harlot. The verse certainly raises some fundamental questions about the biblical attitude to women and to sexuality, (see below, ch. 4, pp. 60f., with notes on p. 136) but it is in no way a simple claim that true Christians must be celibate.

3 Interpreting Revelation

1. 'That Patmos must have been a damned desolate island.' – Quotation from A. Brink. *States of Emergency* in Roger Williamson (ed), *The End in Sight?*, Conference Report of the Life and Peace Institute, Uppsala 1993, p. 116.

2. For a thorough and illuminating examination of John's use of the Old Testament, on which this book has drawn substantially, see Steve Moyise, *The Old Testament in the Book of Revelation*, Sheffield Academic Press 1995.

3. John 4.22; cf. Rom. 9.4–5.

4. The letter to the Hebrews expresses this especially clearly; see Heb. 1.1–2a, which is a summary of the letter's fundamental contention that Christ is God's final word. But the New Testament throughout presents Christ as the fulfilment of Old Testament promises, either by direct quotation (particularly obvious in Matthew's Gospel, but also frequent in Paul) or by presenting Christ in Old Testament terms (sometimes, for

example, using language of Christ that is used of God in the Old Testament).

5. Apocalyptic writing in the Old Testament is to be found in the book of Daniel, and in particular passages in prophets such as Zechariah and Joel. It is a development of prophecy (as can be seen in the book of Ezekiel); this development mostly occurs after the end of the Old Testament period. For a general introduction to the subject of apocalyptic, see D. S. Russell, *Divine Disclosure: An Introduction to Jewish Apocalyptic*, SCM Press 1992.

6. The Antichrist in the New Testament only appears under that name in the epistles of John (I John 2.18 etc., II John 7); but there are figures who represent final opposition to Christ in II Thess. 2.3–10 and Mark 13.22. Similar opponents of God appearing just before the end-time are found in Jewish apocalyptic.

7. A triangular number is one in which consecutive numbers are added: the series goes 1, 3, 6, 10 etc., so that 10, for example, is the triangle of 4, i.e. is the fourth number in the series. A doubly triangular number is the triangle of a triangular number, in this case 666 being the triangle of 36, which is the triangle of 8.

8. For readers who wish to pursue the use of number in Revelation, see Bauckham, *Climax of Prophecy*, pp. 384–407. (Number is also included in Prévost's *How to Read the Apocalypse*; see the next note.)

9. For more on colour in Revelation, see Jean-Pierre Prévost, *How to Read the Apocalypse*, SCM Press 1993, pp.27–29. The whole book is a helpfully presented introduction to Revelation for the non-specialist.

10. This is Hal Lindsey's reading of Rev. 9.17 in *There's a New World Coming: A Prophetic Odyssey*, quoted in Paul Boyer, *When Time Shall Be No More*, Harvard 1992. The latter is an interesting study of the influence of what Boyer calls 'the hidden world of prophecy belief' on modern American culture.

11. Leonard Hodgson, *For Faith and Freedom*, SCM Press 1968, vol. II, pp. 15–16.

12. See, e.g., E. Schüssler Fiorenza, *The Book of Revelation: justice and judgement*, Fortress Press 1984, and, written in the midst of the struggle against apartheid in South Africa, Allan Boesak's *Comfort and Protest*, Saint Andrew Press 1987.

13. Walter Wink, *Naming the Powers*, 1984; *Unmasking the Powers*, 1986; *Engaging the Powers*, 1992; all published by Fortress Press.

14. Wink, *Naming the Powers*, p. 104.
15. Wink, *Unmasking the Powers*, p. 70.
16. Wink, *Naming the Powers*, p. 105.
17. This is a repeated description for God in Revelation: see 1.4, 8; 4.8. In 11.17 and 16.5 the 'is to come' is omitted, but only because at those points God has already come and is acting accordingly.
18. If we follow Mazzaferri in supposing that John saw himself as the final prophet, then this would be a strong argument for deciding that John did expect the End literally to be soon. But most commentators have not taken this view.

4 Can we Accept Revelation?

1. The writings of the New Testament circulated among early Christian churches long before an approved list (or 'canon') was finally decided towards the end of the fourth century. Before that there were different listings of accepted scriptures in different parts of the church; and several lists in the Eastern part of the church excluded Revelation, largely because of suspicion about its use by millenarianists (people expecting the imminent end of the world in a way deemed heretical by the mainstream church).
2. Austin Farrer, *A Rebirth of Images*, Dacre Press 1949.
3. G. B. Caird, *The Revelation of St John the Divine*, A. & C. Black 1966, pp. 74–75.
4. Deciding whether the references to persecution in Revelation are to what is actually happening, or to what has happened in the past and might happen again is partly a matter of deciding on the date of the book. Most scholars date it to the end of the first century for reasons of 'external' evidence (i.e. evidence from outside the book of Revelation itself), when almost certainly persecution was only scattered and sporadic, and most Christians were safe if they lay low. There is a good discussion of the background in John Sweet's very helpful commentary on Revelation (*Revelation*, SCM Press 1979, pp. 21–35); Sweet suggests that John saw his churches as being in danger not so much of persecution, but of colluding with pagan society (and so avoiding persecution).
5. See Steve Moyise, *The Old Testament in the Book of Revelation*, Sheffield Academic Press 1995, pp. 123–35, for a discussion of 'Revelation and the Old Testament in Dialogue', especially pp. 128–30 on the Lamb.

6. See, e.g., Isa. 63.3, 6, and consult the commentaries on other Old Testament use of harvest imagery to describe judgment.

7. Anthony T. Hanson, *The Wrath of the Lamb*, SPCK 1957, ch. 7; the quotation is from p. 160. Hanson understands the 'wrath' in Paul (particularly in Romans 1) in much the same way, in which he is at one with C. H. Dodd, one of the classic commentators on Romans. More recent commentators have questioned whether the 'wrath' can be quite as impersonal as that. See the discussion that follows in the text.

8. With a typical Jewish reluctance to name the name of God, John normally describes these disasters using the passive form of the verb, e.g. 'every mountain and island was removed from its place' (6.14). But there is no intention to leave it unclear who is responsible.

9. This is characteristically signalled by John's noting that people did *not* repent, e.g. at 9.20–21 and 16.9.

10. See, for example, Maurice Wiles, *God's Action in the World*, SCM Press 1986, especially ch. 3.

11. This exercise of individual judgment is, of course, a very Protestant approach to scripture – though many Protestants would want immediately to say that the Bible's judgment of us is what really matters. 'Liberal' Protestants have much to learn both from them and from the Catholic awareness of how fundamentally the Bible is a book of the church. Individuals are easily misguided.

12. See, e.g., Job 10; Ps. 44.9–19, Jer. 20.7.

13. Kenneth Surin, *Theology and the Problem of Evil*, Blackwell 1986.

14. The 'Enlightenment' is a shorthand term for a philosophical movement of the seventeenth and eighteenth centuries in the West which laid great stress on reason and observation of the natural world as the sources of knowledge; it laid the foundation for modern science, and for secularism (though not all those who have been influenced by it have rejected Christian belief).

15. For Jezebel see 2.20ff., and for Babylon 16.17–19.4.

16. See, for example, Isa. 1.21, Jer. 3.1–10, Ezek. 16, Hosea 2–4.

17. See Tina Pippin, 'The Revelation to John', ch. 7 in *Searching the Scriptures: a Feminist Commentary* ed Elisabeth Schüssler Fiorenza, SCM Press 1995, vol. II, pp. 109ff., for a survey of feminist comment on Revelation. Pippin's conclusion is that Revelation 'is not liberating for women readers' (p. 119) and that 'women will testify to a different apocalyptic vision, a

different utopia' (p.127). Though many readers will find some of the exegesis unconvincing (for example, seeing the entry of the [male] faithful into the heavenly city/Bride in terms of mass intercourse), the chapter as a whole expresses very sharply how 'masculine' many of Revelation's thought-forms and values are.

18. Mary Grey, *The Wisdom of Fools?*, SPCK 1993, p. 110.

19. Johan Galtung, 'The Challenge of Religion' in *True to This Earth: Global Challenges and Transforming Faith* ed Alan Race and Roger Williamson, One World Publications 1995.

20. See Richard Bauckham, *The Theology of the Book of Revelation*, CUP 1993, ch. 2 and especially pp. 43–47. The book is an excellent theological study without being over-technical.

21. See 1.5, 7.14, 22.14. It is important that in 22.14 the present participle is used: there is a continuing maintenance of the relationship established in baptism – and correspondingly a continuing danger of letting the relationship lapse and 'soiling' one's clothes (3.4).

22. M. Rissi in *The Future of the World*, ET SCM Press 1972, draws attention to the use of the phrase 'the first resurrection' in 20.6. Is there a hint that there might be a second, after the second death? (It would be strange for death to have the last word.)

23. Luke 6.26; Matt. 5.11.

5 A Vision for the World

1. See, as well as Gen. 2 for the first garden and Isa. 60.3, 11, 19 for the nations entering the city, Isa. 62.3–5 for Zion as the bride of God; and Ezek. 47.1–12 for the life-giving river and the trees bearing monthly fruit.

2. The discussion in chapter four of the vision in which John hears of a Lion and sees a Lamb (see above, pp. 47ff.) has already shown the importance of the relationship between what is heard and what is seen. These are not two different things, but the same thing from different perspectives. See John Sweet's useful explanation of the heard as the theological truth/inner reality and the seen as the outward reality (*Revelation*, pp. 125, 149).

3. See above, pp. 60f. and n. 17 on pp. 136f.

4. 'Both small and great' is a stock phrase for John. See 11.18; 13.16; 19.5, 18; 20.12.

5. See 20.6, and cf. 1.6, 22.5.

6. See 11.13, but cf. 9.21; 15.9,11,21.

7. See 13.12–15; the 'beast whose mortal wound was healed'

would suggest the Roman emperor Nero to John's original readers, who would have been aware of the story that he had returned after his death.

8. See 6.15–17.

9. See 11.7; 13.7, 15.

10. For a discussion of heaven as the place where ultimately reality is seen, see above pp. 42f.

11. For Paul's understanding of the wrath of God, see especially Rom. 1.18–2.10; and for the appreciation that all of creation is caught up in human sinfulness, Rom. 8.18–23. For a thorough discussion of Paul on the wrath of God, see Hanson, *The Wrath of the Lamb*, pp. 68–111.

12. This widely-used phrase is originally from the title of a book by Frank Kermode, *The Sense of an Ending: Studies in the Theory of Fiction*, OUP 1966.

13. See 6.16 for the (unavailing) cry to be hidden from 'the wrath of the Lamb'.

14. Apart from the passage just quoted, judgment and punishment are chiefly in the hands of God, though the Lamb is present in 14.10 where the worshippers of the beast drink the wine of God's wrath. If we are right about the meaning of the opening of the scrolls in 6.1ff. (see above p. 27, with n. 19 on p. 132), we cannot suppose that the Lamb's action is responsible for the unleashing of the judgments. His conquering of the ten kings in 17.14 is not described; what it is supposed to entail will depend on the reader's general conclusions about how warlike a figure the Lamb is. See the discussion in chapter four (pp. 48ff.), which notes the ambivalence of the passage about the Word of God who treads the wine-press of the fury of the wrath of God (19.11–16).

15. See 7.14; 14.1;15.2–3; 19.14.

6 *Worship: Learning to See*

1. Of course human beings are not the only worshippers in Revelation. In the key worship visions of chapters 4 and 5 the whole creation worships, and that is entirely consonant with John's concern with the whole of heaven and earth. If we concentrate in this chapter on human worship, that is because the worship of the non-human creation can, as it were, be taken as given. The worship of human beings most certainly cannot.

2. See 19.10; 22.8–9. Reverence paid to heavenly messengers is a

stock feature of apocalyptic writing, but the response is not usually so uncompromising.

3. Wisdom 11.24.

4. Revelation here is within a strong biblical tradition of God's ultimate judgment reversing earthly experience. Psalm 73 is a good Old Testament example (see especially v.17 for the 'end' of the wicked); the Beatitudes (Matt. 5.3–12, Luke 6.20–23) give the positive side of the reward of the godly poor.

5. For a discussion of John's attitude to God's punishment of sinners, see above, ch. 4, p. 53.

6. One of the earliest known prayers after communion ends, 'Let grace come, and let this world pass. Hosanna to the God of David. If any is holy, let him come; if any is not holy, let him repent. Maranatha [Aramaic for "Our Lord, come"]. Amen' (*Didache*, or, *Teaching of the Twelve Apostles*, quoted in H. Bettenson (ed), *Documents of the Christian Church*, 2nd edn, OUP 1963, p. 65).

7. See above ch. 2, pp. 25f., 30.

8. We have argued in ch. 5 (pp. 69f.) that Revelation is basically 'pro-earth'. But this is a matter of God's ultimate will for the earth, not of his judgment on its present state. Indeed, if his ultimate will is to be fulfilled, judgment on earth's present state is positively required.

9. For the Antichrist, see above ch. 3, p. 35., with n. 6 on p. 134.

10. See P. S. Minear's careful examination in 'The Kings of the Earth' in *I Saw a New Earth*, Corpus Books, Washington 1968.

11. The devil falsely claims the worship which is ultimately due to God the Father. The first beast parodies Christ in representing the dragon as Christ does the Father (and in rising from the sea, which is an image of the resurrection). The second beast apes the Holy Spirit in producing great signs and fire from heaven, as well as being the false prophet described in the text. For the Satanic trinity elsewhere in Revelation, see 16.13 where they cause three foul spirits to permeate the whole earth, assembling God's enemies for the final battle, and 19.20 and 20.10, where they are finally destroyed.

12. John 16.13.

13. An interesting commentary from India on Revelation (B. Wielenga, *Revelation to John*, TTS Publications 1989), which sees the marks of the first beast in the political/economic power of multinationals, sees the second as involving in its propaganda machinery 'intellectuals, artists, professors, teachers, journalists, all sorts of people' (p. 54).

14. See, e.g., Rex Ambler, *Global Theology*, SCM Press 1990, pp. 20–22.
15. Ulrich Duchrow, *Alternatives to Global Capitalism*, International Books, The Netherlands 1995, p. 70.
16. Ibid., p. 228.
17. For 'our natural inclinations and material interests', see the Methodist Covenant Service, *Methodist Worship Book*, Methodist Publishing House 1999, pp. 288, 289.
18. This point is made by Charles Elliott in his book *Praying the Kingdom*, Darton, Longman and Todd 1985, p. 135. The book is profoundly helpful in bringing 'the world' into both public and private prayer.
19. From Isaac Watts' hymn, *The Lord Jehovah reigns*.

7 Witness: Communicating the Vision

1. Rom. 15.20, cf. 1.5.
2. Mark 13.10; Matt. 28.19.
3. I Tim. 6.13.
4. The originator of this theory was a philosopher named Jeremy Bentham (1748–1831), but it was modified and given its name by John Stuart Mill (1806–73), whose book *Utilitarianism* is the best place to start.
5. The word 'deontological' is derived from the Greek 'dei', which means 'it is necessary'.
6. Mazzaferri (*Genre of the Book of Revelation*), whose work broke new ground in the study of Revelation in terms of prophecy, takes the view that it is John himself as prophet who sums up the whole of past prophecy, but he has not been generally followed.
7. C. S. Lewis, *Mere Christianity*, Collins Fontana 1952, pp. 102–3.
8. This has not always been true: institutional authority has often been respected regardless of whether individuals were speaking from personal experience or not. But such respect is not a characteristic of today's Western society, even within institutions, as the Roman Catholic Church's experience in the matter of contraception might suggest. This is not to deny that people who command great personal respect may well be listened to quite outside the field of their own personal experience, in this age as in any other.
9. How we try to behave (which is what 'ethics' is about) is not only a question of the principles on which we act, but of the values we

have. 'Gospel values' is precisely the right phrase for Christians: what we think of as important depends on what we see God as being and doing for us.

8 *Following the Lamb*

1. Whether to say 'Church' or 'church' is a tricky question, because the word can be used to refer to different groups (anything from a single congregation to an invisible body of all Christians whose boundaries are known only to God), and it can also carry very different theological understandings. In this book we have used 'church' in general, to cover a range of different understandings, reserving 'Church' for those cases where it is clear that the universal (catholic) Church is intended.
2. Stanley Hauerwas and William H. Willimon, *Resident Aliens*, Abingdon Press, Nashville 1992, p. 27. The exact quotation is 'Alas, in leaning over to speak to the modern world, we had fallen in.' The preceding sentence makes soberingly clear what may be at stake in over-accommodating to the world: 'If Caesar (i.e. state power) can get Christians there to swallow the "Ultimate Solution", and Christians here to embrace the bomb, there is no limit to what we will not do for the modern world.'
3. Mark 10.43.
4. Rom. 12.2.
5. John 17.11, 15–16.
6. Note in the Gospels the testing of Jesus alone in the wilderness as preparation for his ministry, and his lone vigil in Gethsemane before his saving death. Cf. Hebrews, which strikingly insists that Christ as high priest is *both* 'separated from sinners' (7.26) *and* 'like his brothers and sisters in every respect' (2.17).
7. Eph. 4.11.
8. An example of prayer material which uses pictorial images to great effect is *Dear Life*, Christian Aid 1998.
9. In *Alternatives to Global Capitalism*, Duchrow suggests specific ways in which the church can respond to the present world economic system with a mixture of resistance, development of small-scale economic alternatives and political pressure. It is of course possible to engage with the issue personally in terms of life-style, and many individual Christians do so (though many do not). But it is what the church should do corporately that we are focussing on here.